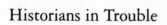

Historians in Trouble

Also by Jon Wiener

Gimme Some Truth: The John Lennon FBI Files
Come Together: John Lennon in His Time
Professors, Politics, and Pop
Social Origins of the New South

Historians in Trouble

Plagiarism, Fraud, and Politics in the Ivory Tower

JON WIENER

THE NEW PRESS

NEW YORK
LONDON

*554 88166

Requests for permission to reproduce selections from this book
should be mailed to: Permissions Department,
The New Press, 38 Greene Street, New York, NY 10013

Published in the United States by The New Press, New York, 2005
Distributed by W. W. Norton & Company, Inc., New York

LIBRARY OF CONGRESS CATALOGING-IN-PUBLICATION DATA

Wiener, Jon.
  Historians in trouble : plagiarism, fraud, and politics in the ivory tower / Jon Wiener.
    p. cm.
  Includes bibliographical references and index.
  ISBN 1-56584-884-5
  1. Historians—United States—Biography. 2. Historians—Press coverage—United
States—Case studies. 3. Professional ethics—United States—Case studies. 4. Mass
media—Political aspects—United States—History—20th century. 5. Power (Social
sciences)—United States—Case studies. 6. Historiography—Political aspects—United
States—History—20th century. 7. Plagiarism—United States—History—20th century. 8.
Fraud—United States—History—20th century. 9. United States—Historiography. I. Title.

E175.45.W54 2005
302.23—dc22   2004050431

The New Press was established in 1990 as a not-for-profit alternative to the large,
commercial publishing houses currently dominating the book publishing industry.
The New Press operates in the public interest rather than for private gain, and
is committed to publishing, in innovative ways, works of educational, cultural, and
community value that are often deemed insufficiently profitable.

www.thenewpress.com

Composition by Westchester Book Composition

Printed in the United States of America

2 4 6 8 10 9 7 5 3 1

Contents

Acknowledgments

This book, more than most, is the result of conversations, arguments, and comments from friends. I am grateful especially to Eric Foner, Roy Rosenzweig, Judy Fiskin, Alice Fahs, Jan Lewis, and Michael Johnson, each of whom generously read a full draft of the manuscript and provided invaluable guidance and help.

For conversations and arguments about historians in trouble, I thank Joyce Appleby, Jean Agnew, David Nasaw, Ronald Steel, Vanessa Schwartz, and Linda Gordon. I thought about each of them a lot while I was writing this. I also relied on help from Leon Litwack, Catherine Clinton, Michael Bellesiles, and Ira Berlin. Rick Shenkman has done me (and the profession) an invaluable service with his History News Network, even if I have complained to him about specific postings.

Several of the chapters here appeared originally in a different form in America's Oldest Weekly. I am deeply indebted to the wonderful editors at *The Nation* who encouraged me to pursue these stories and then worked to help me get them right: first of all Victor Navasky and Katrina vanden Heuvel, and also John Leonard, Art Winslow, Elsa Dixler, Karen Rothmyer, Hillary Frey, and Roane Carey. At the late lamented *Lingua Franca,* I also had terrific editors: Margaret Talbot, Judith Shulevitz, and Alex Star.

In my writing, I have been inspired by the exemplary work of some other friends: Marc Cooper, Harold Meyerson, Katha Pollitt, Adam Shatz, and Robert Scheer—each provided an irresistible model of how to argue and how to write.

At UCI, very special thanks go to Vicki Ruiz, Ken Pomeranz, Jim Given, Mark Poster, and Sharon Block, as well as Alice Fahs.

Several chapters here are dependent largely on interviews. On the Stephan Thernstrom case, I am indebted to many people for agreeing to talk on the record: Orlando Patterson, Fred Jewett, Phyllis Keller, John Womack, Martin Kilson, and Stephan Thernstrom himself.

On the Michael Bellesiles case, I thank Garry Wills, Mary Beth Norton, Michael Zuckerman, Michael Kammen, Matt Warshauer, and Michael Bellesiles himself. I am also indebted to Lee Formwalt, Tom Bender, Chris Grasso, James Henretta, Jonathan Prude, James Roark, Don Higgenbotham, Eric Monkkonen, Stanley Kutler, and Lynn Hunt.

On the David Abraham case, I am grateful for the help of the late Lawrence Stone, Natalie Davis, Carl Schorske, Timothy Tackett, Gerald Feldman, Stanley Katz, Robert Tignor, and David Abraham himself.

On the Mike Davis case, I thank Kevin Starr, Lewis MacAdams, the late Michael Sprinker, D.J. Waldie, Sue Horton, Richard Walker, and Mike Davis himself.

On the Allen Weinstein case, I am grateful for the help of Garry Wills, Victor Navasky, William Reuben, Ronald Grele, Dennis Bilger, and Allen Weinstein himself.

For the chapter on Denmark Vesey, I am indebted to Michael

Johnson, Ira Berlin, Peter Wood, Drew Faust, Joanne Meyerowitz, John Bowles, P. Bruce Pipes, and Edward Pearson.

On the Dino Cinel case, I thank David Nasaw, Jason Berry, Ernst Benjamin, Richard Gid Powers, Irwin Polishook, and Sandi Cooper.

Thanks also to the archivists at the DeKalb County Courthouse, Atlanta, Georgia, and the Southern Historical Collection at the University of North Carolina library, and to archivist Dennis Bilger at the Truman Library.

I am also indebted to fellow panelists who discussed historians in trouble at history conventions: at the 2004 AHA meeting in Washington D.C., James Banner and Rick Shenkman, and at the 2003 OAH meeting in Memphis, Paul Finkelman and Ralph Luker.

The New Press was wonderful: Colin Robinson's enthusiasm got this book going, and Abby Aguirre's persistence got it done. Sarah Fan solved problems with admirable calm.

I owe a special debt to the immensely talented and resourceful Eileen Luhr, who successfully checked notes that seemed uncheckable and saved me from many inexcusable errors. Those that remain are, of course, my own responsibility.

Many of the people named here disagree with at least some of what I've written, and none of them agrees with all of it. But if I manage to avoid becoming a historian in trouble myself, it's only because of their help.

Historians in Trouble

Introduction:
Historians in Trouble

*H*istorians have been in the news a lot recently, and the news has not been good—accusations of plagiarism, investigations of research fraud, and punishments for classroom misconduct have made headlines and in some cases even ended up in court.[1] Media spectacles around scholarly scandals have become, as Ron Robin writes, "a veritable cottage industry"; investigations of misconduct that in the past were confined to the profession, to academic senate committees and academic journals, now are reported on page one and on TV news. What's new, he argues, is not the uncovering of wrongdoing, but rather the visibility of the charges, and their dissemination as media events—"performances, staged and choreographed for mass-mediated consumption."[2]

But not all cases of wrongdoing by historians follow this scenario.

While some charges of misconduct end up on page one and bring careers to an end, other equally serious charges stay out of the media spotlight and bring little or no public sanction or punishment. Why do some cases become media events while others remain within the confines of scholarly settings?

The answer briefly is power—especially power wielded by groups outside the history profession. Historians targeted by powerful outside groups can face intense media scrutiny and severe sanctions for transgressions, while historians connected to powerful outside groups can be shielded from the media spotlight as well as from the consequences of malfeasance; in some cases, they have even been rewarded.

This book investigates the relationships between power and media spectacles by examining a dozen key cases involving historians. The cases range across the political spectrum and represent a variety of charges of misconduct. They do not, I must emphasize, fall into a single pattern or point to single conclusion. Some divide along left-right lines, while others do not. The cases illustrate the many different ways that power has been deployed in media spectacles to highlight the pitfalls of certain ways of writing history. They also illustrate the ways other cases have been neglected or ignored by the media. They show the different ways organized pressure groups have taken action against authors they regard as enemies. All of the cases shed light on the question of what happens to scholars charged with violating standards or rules, and in each case I try to explain its particular outcome.

The point here is not to condone misconduct or make excuses for errors. As E.H. Carr wrote in his classic book *What Is History?*, "accuracy is a duty, not a virtue."[3] The point is rather to explore why some instances are punished severely and others not at all.

George W. Bush's recent nominations and appointments of historians to the National Council on the Humanities and the National Archives provide illuminating cases of the uses of power in the face of charges of misconduct. Elizabeth Fox-Genovese, who teaches history at Emory University, is a prominent critic of the contemporary feminist movement and the author of the book *Feminism Is Not the Story of My Life.* In 1995, she was sued for violating the civil rights of a female subordinate. In the lawsuit, the plaintiff, a middle-aged woman who had been a graduate student of, and assistant to, Fox-Genovese, declared that she had been verbally abused and asked to perform duties that would not have been asked of a male subordinate—like picking up Fox-Genovese's laundry and walking her dog. The court proceedings received considerable press coverage, and in 1996, before the case went to the jury, Emory settled it for an undisclosed sum—reported to be $1 million. Despite Fox-Genovese's heavily documented record of misconduct, Emory did not conduct its own disciplinary proceedings, and in 2003 the Bush White House awarded Fox-Genovese the National Humanities Medal.

Allen Weinstein, in his book *Perjury,* did more to document the case against Alger Hiss than any other historian. But his documentation was challenged; many key interviewees insisted they had been misquoted. He steadfastly refused to make the documentation available to other historians, as required by the American Historical Association (AHA) guidelines—and as Michael Bellesiles and others accused of misconduct did. Nevertheless, Weinstein faced no investigations or penalties; the AHA refused to take up the case against him. The mainstream media ignored the charges—perhaps because Weinstein is on the popular side of an old debate; he defended the conventional wisdom about Alger Hiss. The people who have questioned the book's documentation did not have the power to get their case into the mainstream media—partly because the mainstream does not want to have to deal with the possibility that something is seriously wrong with the leading work documenting Hiss's guilt. Allen Weinstein stonewalled his critics for twenty-five years; then, in 2004, George W. Bush nominated him to be Archivist of the United States.

A third case: Stephan Thernstrom teaches history at Harvard and has been a prominent critic of affirmative action, writing that blacks are to blame for many of their educational problems and suggesting that there is little racism in America today. A decade ago, some black students complained that he had been "racially insensitive" in his lectures. Thernstrom's outraged counterattack made him a hero in right-wing circles. His defense was featured in *New York* magazine and in Dinesh D'Souza's 1991 book, *Illiberal Education,* which spent nine weeks on the bestseller list. C. Vann Woodward, writing in the *New York Review of Books,* explained the Thernstrom case as an example of "the attack on freedom . . . led by minorities."

In fact, there had been no "attack on freedom" at Harvard. Three black students had complained about a single lecture—a story reported in the campus newspaper. Thernstrom responded in the national media with the false claim that the Harvard administration had colluded with black students to make him a victim of "McCarthyism of the left." In 2002, the Bush White House nominated Thernstrom to the National Council on the Humanities.

The controversies around Fox-Genovese, Weinstein, and Thernstrom became media events, but their supporters succeeded for the most part in portraying the central figures not as miscreants guilty of misconduct but rather as innocent victims of "political correctness." All were honored for "standing up to the left" and rewarded with White House nominations to distinguished positions. In each of these cases, the crucial issue was who had the power to frame the media spectacle.

While these historians' careers advanced despite charges of misconduct, others faced very different outcomes. The most obvious contrast is found in the media spectacle around Michael Bellesiles, the Emory historian who wrote about the origins of gun culture in America. He faced a vociferous campaign by gun rights groups, which prompted debate in scholarly journals and then an investigation by distinguished historians. In the end, he resigned a tenured position—even though the Emory review panel found evidence of fraud only on one table that was referred to only a few times in a 400-page book. Bellesiles made a strong case that he was guilty of error but not fraud. The episode demonstrated the power of an organized political group on the right to target a historian they identified as an enemy and raises the question of the appropriate sanction for error.

Mike Davis provides a second example of a media spectacle around a historian targeted by the right for his politics. Davis, a leading Marxist historian, won a MacArthur "genius" grant and an appointment as a Getty Institute scholar for his book on Los Angeles, *City of Quartz,* after which a Malibu realtor launched a campaign in 1999 charging that his footnotes in a new book, *Ecology of Fear,* were fraudulent. The charges mushroomed and were featured in the *New York Times,* the *Economist,* and on page one of the *Los Angeles Times*; neither UCLA nor USC would hire him; he ended up leaving Los Angeles, for a job at SUNY-Stony Brook. Evidently, the search committee and administration at Stony Brook concluded that the errors in his footnotes were minor and that he met the requirements for appointment to a tenured position.

The recent stories of Bellesiles and Mike Davis were reminiscent in some ways of the David Abraham case of the mid-eighties, when an assistant professor coming up for tenure at Princeton faced attack by a politically conservative senior Yale historian whose work he had challenged. The issue, as presented by the media: errors in Abraham's account of German business backing for Hitler. Abraham had the support of many leading historians, but the "Abraham case" was featured on page one of the *New York Times,* and within a year, he was forced out of the profession. These cases suggest the right has had much more power than the left to define the meaning and significance of charges of misconduct for the public.

But not all recent charges of scholarly misconduct became media spectacles and ended up on page one of the *Times.* The third section of this book examines cases where the charges of misconduct were significant and where the evidence was strong, but nevertheless these cases were greeted with indifference by the media.

John Lott's research on guns has played a key role in leading states and cities to pass laws permitting people to carry concealed firearms. Lott argued that "brandishing" guns without firing them was sufficient to deter criminals in almost all cases. But his claim to have done survey research on this issue was shown to be fraudulent. Nevertheless, Lott received virtually no media attention for this fraud and paid no penalties; his publisher, the University of Chicago Press, has kept the fraudulent claims in the new edition of the book, Lott continues to publish op-eds in leading venues, and the "brandishing" laws he helped pass remain in force.

Edward A. Pearson's 1999 book on the Denmark Vesey slave rebellion was shown to contain massive errors of transcription and, more seriously, a deeply erroneous description of the document he transcribed: it was not, as Pearson said, a verbatim "trial transcript," but rather a retrospective summary of testimony for the prosecution, revised by persons unknown to us. This misunderstanding, in the view of many, undermined the author's entire thesis and suggested that Denmark Vesey was an innocent man framed by the white power structure rather than the leader of a slave rebellion. The book's publisher withdrew it from publication. But no other disciplinary action was taken against Pearson. At Franklin and Marshall College, where he teaches, the administration reviewed his case and decided no punishment by the school was appropriate. He remains chair of the History Department at Franklin and Marshall.

These cases raise the question, why do some charges of misconduct become media spectacles, with dramatic consequences for the central figures, while others do not? The explanation seems to lie in the power, or lack of power, of interested constituencies. In the case of Pearson, there is simply no constituency in or outside the profession arguing that a key slave rebellion should be removed from the historical record. And the Lott case illustrates the way the gun lobby has immensely more power than the gun-control lobby.

Finally, I want to consider media spectacles that were not framed around a left-right confrontation:

The Dino Cinel case was one of the first in which sexual abuse by a Catholic priest became known (in 1993) and is still one of the best documented. After Cinel was appointed distinguished professor of Italian-American immigration history at the City University of New York, the media discovered he had been defrocked as a priest several years earlier for having had sex with a number of teenage boys. Nevertheless, the American Federation of Teachers, which represented Cinel, argued he should not be fired—because he had tenure. As a result, it took years to dismiss him from the university.

Joseph Ellis, the bestselling and Pulitzer Prize–winning historian, made page one in 2001 for lying to his class at Mount Holyoke, telling students he had fought in Vietnam. Mount Holyoke's punishment was strong and appropriate. But the argument made in the media was that lying to students in class is not as serious as lying to readers in print, and thus he was promptly rehabilitated by the *New York Times* and the *New Yorker*.

Plagiarism provides the simplest case of scholarly misconduct and the easiest to explain to the public. Thus the well-known cases of plagiarism by the late Stephen Ambrose and by Doris Kearns Goodwin became major media spectacles. Plagiarism provides the easiest case to adjudicate because the evidence is clear-cut; but, as Thomas Mallon showed in his 1989 book on the topic, some of the most blatant cases received the least attention and the lightest punishment.[4] Here the size of the spectacle seems to depend on the celebrity of the accused rather than the seriousness of the offense.

My concluding chapter addresses some obvious questions: is some kind of stricter oversight of the history profession necessary; and if so, who should exercise it? Charges of misconduct that become media spectacles have ended careers only when powerful groups outside the profession organize campaigns that demand punishment. Typically, the right rather than the left has organized, and succeeded with, such campaigns. Could the history profession itself counter the power of these organized interest groups? The American Historical Association recently abandoned its procedures for addressing charges of plagiarism and professional misconduct. That gives the media, and the forces that shape them, even more power to define the issues and adjudicate scholarly controversies, to honor scholars who advance their partisan political agendas and punish those who challenge those agendas.

I

Presidential Nominees

1

Feminism and Harassment: Elizabeth Fox-Genovese Goes to Court

When President George W. Bush awarded Elizabeth Fox-Genovese the National Humanities Medal at the White House in November 2003, her bio on the official government website reported that, among her achievements, she was the founding director of the Institute for Women's Studies at Emory University.[1] The White House did not note the story about Fox-Genovese that had run in the *Atlanta Journal-Constitution* in 1996: "With jurors waiting in the wings and a camera from CBS' '48 Hours' ready to roll, lawyers reached a settlement Thursday afternoon in the case of a nationally known Emory University historian accused of sexually harassing and discriminating against a former protégé."[2]

Dozens of prominent historians were prepared to testify against Fox-Genovese in court when Emory University decided not to defend her against charges of sexual harassment and discrimination. Nevertheless, seven years later she was honored by President Bush. How did she do it? The answer lies partly in the title of the book she published the same year the lawsuit was settled: *Feminism Is Not the Story of My Life*. Fox-Genovese turned herself into a right-wing victim of feminist political correctness, a person who stood up to the feminists and their friends—and thus a person to be honored by the Republican White House.

The woman who sued Fox-Genovese was Virginia Gould—described in the press as "a middle-aged mother of four" who had worked for Fox-Genovese as associate director of that same Institute for Women's Studies. Fox-Genovese had been the supervisor on her 1991 Ph.D. dissertation. Gould had charged that Fox-Genovese violated federal civil rights statutes when she demanded that Gould perform without pay personal services that were not required of male subordinates, including picking up her laundry, hosting parties for her, cleaning her house, and walking her dog.[3]

In deciding to settle the case, Emory avoided going to trial where a jury—and the national media—would spend an anticipated six weeks hearing testimony about Fox-Genovese and her treatment of her subordinates and students from more than 100 witnesses. The plaintiff's attorneys were prepared to argue not only that Fox-Genovese treated her assistant with "abuse," "verbal tirades," and "a loud, threatening and personally demeaning voice and manner" that was "deliberate, willful and malicious." They were also prepared to argue that Fox-Genovese had treated other people the same way—other students and faculty at Emory, and also students and faculty at the schools where she had taught previously. The witness list reportedly included some of the nation's leading historians, including C. Vann Woodward and Fox-Genovese's husband, Eugene D. Genovese. The judge told the news media that, since federal civil rights questions were at issue, the case might go all the way to the U.S. Supreme Court.

The settlement amount was confidential, but the *Journal-Constitution* reported that Gould had originally sought $2 million, and had previously rejected an offer of $175,000; the paper concluded that the settlement was "a far cry from both numbers"—that is, Emory paid a lot less than $2 million, but a lot more than $175,000.[4] One elected official of the Organization of American Historians told me the settlement was $1 million.

Fox-Genovese was quoted in the press saying she felt "betrayed" by Emory's decision to settle the case rather than defend her against the charges of sexual discrimination.[5] She had already resigned as director of the Institute for Women's Studies.

Although Emory's settlement conceded the case against Fox-Genovese, the university never held its own disciplinary proceedings regarding her conduct. Abuse of and discrimination against staff and students clearly violates university rules. Emory had investigated and disciplined other faculty members accused of misconduct. In this case, several dozen people, many of them at Emory, had sworn affidavits on file at the county courthouse describing Fox-Genovese's misconduct.[6] The evidence against her may not have been completely accurate, but it made a prima facie case for action by Emory. The university's decision not to consider whether she violated its own rules and principles requires scrutiny.

First, the case against Fox-Genovese: the settlement followed three years of what the press called "take-no-prisoners legal war-fare." The case had been filed in January 1993. The strongest evidence against Fox-Genovese was a 1991 memo written by the assistant vice president for equal opportunity programs, Robert Ethridge, and sent to the dean of the graduate school, Eleanor Main. He wrote that he had talked to staff members in the women's studies department and to students, both past and present. "Each person informed me of the intimidation they endured from Betsey. They expressed how they have had to sponsor parties for her, pick up her laundry and dry cleaning, pay for lunches, teach classes for her without pay" or else "face the possibility of her not signing their dissertation or not writing a positive letter of recommendation." The students, in particular, he wrote, were "afraid that Betsey will do whatever she can to destroy their career in Women's Studies" if they failed to "do her bidding." Key parts of that memo were quoted in the *Atlanta Journal-Constitution.*[7]

The plaintiff's attorneys were prepared to present testimony from some of the people to whom Ethridge had talked. Patricia McGarry worked in the Women's Studies office at Emory. "One would like to think that a person in charge of a Women's Studies Department would be a fair and equal person," she stated in a sworn deposition. "Betsey was not a fair person. I know of many women graduate students who cleaned Betsey's house, and took care of her dog, and yes, threw her parties. It seemed to come with the territory. . . . The choice seemed like either swallow your pride until you got your dissertation signed or become the enemy of the Genoveses. . . . Everyone knew that once you got on the bad side of the

Genoveses that your academic life would end, and not just at Emory. They were people who did not forget."[8]

Lisa Tyree was a graduate student studying under Fox-Genovese. "When I did try to see her, she informed me that she had no time for me and would call me when she needed me and not to call her," Tyree stated in her declaration. "Many times has she called me on the phone, late in the evening, only to belittle and abuse me. She was threatening, accusing that I did owe her complete loyalty. . . . She convinced me that if I did not pay homage, such as taking her to lunch and performing menial duties for her, she would disable me from publishing and discontinue my funding. . . . I was required to be her errand person, housesitter and dogsitter."[9]

Court papers filed by the plaintiff's attorneys indicated they were prepared to call witnesses to testify that Fox-Genovese manipulated her female students into a relationship she herself was said to call "mutually agreed enslavement." That testimony—and that phrase—was to come from Sarah Elbert, a former colleague of Fox-Genovese's in the history department at SUNY-Binghamton. She was quoted in court papers arguing that, in Fox-Genovese's relations with female students, she would "portray herself to them as a 'counselor/therapist' and delve into their personal lives, purporting to be their 'rescuer.' . . . Fox-Genovese told these students that she had the power to keep them from getting jobs and the power to control their futures. Fox-Genovese used these threats to control students and require them to do her bidding, including menial and demeaning tasks."[10]

The central weapon Fox-Genovese deployed when she "took

advantage of the emotional vulnerability" of female grad students, according to the plaintiff's attorneys, was to "manipulate them by threatening not to sign their dissertations." Stephanie McCurry, now a professor at the University of Pennsylvania, had Fox-Genovese as her dissertation advisor at SUNY-Binghamton. "Fox-Genovese's initial review of the dissertation was extremely favorable," her deposition indicated, but after McCurry accepted a job at the University of California, San Diego, "Fox-Genovese became extraordinarily critical of her dissertation, told McCurry that people would laugh at it, and refused to sign it." McCurry told Fox-Genovese that refusing to sign would cause McCurry to lose her job. "Fox-Genovese required McCurry to meet her in a bar, told McCurry that she 'broke her heart.' When McCurry asked her what she was talking about, Fox-Genovese told her, 'don't you know that I love you?'" Eventually, after tearful appeals from McCurry, Fox-Genovese signed her dissertation, but told her "it is no good" and said she needed Fox-Genovese's help "to write the book." (McCurry wrote the book without Fox-Genovese's help, and it won several awards.)[11]

Another weapon Fox-Genovese deployed was the threat to cut funding for grad students. Pat Michelson, former chair of Women's Studies, filed a handwritten affidavit: "student complained to me about abusive treatment" from Fox-Genovese, "that she discriminates in the allocation of funding, that they were bullied," that "Fox-Genovese had 'loyalty tests' which they must adhere to or be subjected to her wrath and their careers ruined." Michelson said she had reported these complaints to the appropriate administrative officials in 1990–91. She listed six students and two faculty members who had complained to her.[12]

A number of other nationally prominent former colleagues were prepared to testify against Fox-Genovese in trial. Melvyn Dubofsky, a well-known historian of American labor, had been chair of the history department at Binghamton; he was on record in court documents saying Fox-Genovese had caused "total chaos" in that department "by fostering jealousy and distrust among faculty and students." Joan Hoff-Wilson is a respected presidential biographer and former executive secretary of the Organization of American Historians. Attorneys said she was ready to testify that Fox-Genovese "frequently tried to harm her professional reputation for no reason other than jealousy." John Chaffee, a prominent historian of China, had also been department chair at Binghamton; he described Fox-Genovese as "always causing trouble. Few people could get along with her. She was frequently in a rage, often 'after someone.' "[13]

Earlier in her career, when Fox-Genovese left Rochester for Binghamton, she was replaced by Bonnie Smith. Smith, now a named chair professor of French history at Rutgers who was nominated to be president of the American Historical Association, said Fox-Genovese had "attempted to sabotage" her career, for no other reason, she thought, than the fact that Smith had been chosen to replace her.[14] William Leach was nominated for the National Book Award for *Land of Desire*; he was described in court documents observing that "Fox-Genovese tries to seduce weak female students to satisfy her needs. Fox-Genovese acts viciously and unpredictably toward those who are dependent on her."[15]

The plaintiff's attorneys also argued that, even before she came to Emory, Fox-Genovese had denied financial aid to students to punish them for failing to defer to her. Debra McGregor was a grad student of Fox-Genovese's at Rochester who "was favored by Fox-Genovese until she announced she was marrying" a fellow student in the program. "Fox-Genovese became furious with both of them and told Debra that she could not have a career if she had children. . . . Within two days of the marriage announcement, Fox-Genovese issued new rules for financial aid. These rules removed Debra and Robert [her fiancé] from funding. Debra, who was pregnant, had a miscarriage the next day. The miscarriage was attributed to the stress caused by Fox-Genovese's actions."[16]

Six colleagues in the Emory history department all stated in sworn depositions that they "had students who came to them complaining of abuse and harassment by Fox-Genovese." The six included Dan T. Carter, author of the classic *Scottsboro: An American Tragedy*; James Roark, who has been Pitt Professor of American History and Institutions at Cambridge University; and Susan Socolow, a named chair professor of Latin American history who had been vice president of the American Historical Association.[17]

The truth of these claims was never tested in open court. Fox-Genovese had prepared a defense, which included her own witnesses as well as challenges to those for the other side. Nevertheless, the record against her is an extraordinary one, which helps explain why Emory preferred to settle rather than defend Fox-Genovese against the testimony from eminent historians and distinguished colleagues. But it does not explain why Emory made no move toward disciplinary proceedings to determine whether Fox-Genovese violated university rules about abusive and discriminatory treatment of staff and students.

Fox-Genovese apparently regarded the case as historically significant—she deposited her records of *Gould v. Emory* at the Southern Historical Collection at the University of North Carolina at Chapel Hill, the country's premier archive of southern history. The collection website lists three boxes of depositions, correspondence, exhibits, and notes about the case. But when I requested permission to read those documents, the head archivist informed me that "our gift agreement with Dr. Fox-Genovese restricts the entire collection from use for twenty-five years."[18] That means they would become available to researchers in 2021.

But since court records are public documents, the papers for *Gould v. Emory* are also archived in the DeKalb County courthouse outside of Atlanta, where the case was heard. One striking document in the county archives is Fox-Genovese's "Motion to Exclude the Dog Training Metaphor." Gould's suit had described Fox-Genovese as aggressive and abusive. The metaphor in question appeared in Fox-Genovese's 1991 book *Feminism Without Illusions*. It began, "I am the proud mistress of a very large dog named Josef." The problem was how to train him. Originally "I, having been raised to think like a girl, mistakenly thought that the appropriate way to deal with a young creature, a mere puppy, was to be gentle and speak softly—to nurture and cultivate this fledgling personality.

I was wrong." She eventually learned that "the only way to train a dog is to establish yourself as master"—to use what she called "a certain amount of brute force":

> I had to learn to raise my voice and to adopt a severe, commanding tone. I had to learn to pick him up by his jowls and deck him, flat out on his back. At the worst, I had to learn to put on heavy leather gloves and to drag him out from under the table, where he was baring his forbidding teeth, in order to deck him again. Above all, I had to learn that I could never afford to lose a confrontation with him. In short, I had to win. . . . I learned something I could never have imagined about the pleasures of winning without guilt. The lesson has stayed with me.[19]

"The metaphor is wholly irrelevant" to the issues in the case, Fox-Genovese's attorneys argued.[20] In her own deposition, Fox-Genovese argued that the dog-training metaphor was "not a blueprint for dealing with human beings." And even if was such a blueprint, her attorneys argued, it could not be evidence about sexual discrimination, because "it could just as easily apply to men as to women."[21]

The most peculiar and confusing part of Gould's lawsuit was the "sexual harassment" claim. Gould's complaint declared that, after Fox-Genovese "engaged in a verbal tirade of abuse," she often "demanded that Dr. Gould provide a sexual favor in that Defendant Fox-Genovese asked Dr. Gould to give her a physical caress."[22] This was not a claim that Fox-Genovese demanded lesbian sex with Virginia Gould. Gould's complaint was that Fox-Genovese demanded "a hug" from her after shouting at her—hugs Gould did not want to provide—and that these hugs became a requirement of the job. She argued that these were "unwelcome" demands, which fit the legal definition of sexual harassment that creates a hostile work environment.

Fox-Genovese's attorneys argued strenuously on this point on the one day the court held open hearings on the case—May 24, 1995. The issue at hand was the defendants' motion for summary judgment, so the defense—Fox-Genovese—went first. Emory attorney Skip Hudgins told the court that the plaintiff, Virginia Gould, "was not the subject of unwelcome harassment. . . . Where there are mixed signals, where there's no clear evidence given as to what conduct is being accepted or not accepted by the person who's claiming to be harassed, you are not subject to a claim for sexual harassment." He said, "The same person who says she was subject to sexual harassment is the person who . . . frequently hugged Dr. Fox-Genovese without protest while a graduate student, and while employed as associate director."[23] He went on to reject each of Gould's other claims.

Next, Fox-Genovese's personal attorney, David Tisinger, took up the issue of intentional infliction of emotional harm. He told the court the prevailing legal standard held that "the conduct has to be so outrageous in character and so extreme in degree as to go beyond all possible bounds of decency, and to be regarded as atrocious and utterly intolerable in a civilized community." He said that an impartial observer would conclude that Fox-Genovese's conduct was not that bad.[24]

Then Gould's attorney, Patrick McKee, spoke. He opened by

reading to the court the letter written by Assistant Vice-President Robert W. Ethridge to Dean Eleanor Main, the one that described how Fox-Genovese's students and staff complained to him that "they have had to sponsor parties for her, pick up her laundry/dry cleaning, pay for lunches, teach classes for her without pay, and generally do her bidding, or face the possibility of her not signing their dissertation or not writing a positive letter of recommendation."[25]

Then he took up the issue of sexual harassment. The defense had suggested that Gould "accepted" Fox-Genovese's demands for "hugs"; McKee replied by citing testimony from Gould that, when she complained to Ethridge about those demands, he himself told her that, in his opinion as the person charged with enforcing federal nondiscrimination laws at Emory, she was being sexually harassed. He handed her a videotape on sexual harassment and told her to go home and watch it.

Gould's attorney then took up the issue of retaliation by Emory, because, after Gould complained to the administration about Fox-Genovese, Gould was fired. Next he argued the "negligent hiring" claim—that Emory should have known about Fox-Genovese's history of misconduct at Rochester and Binghamton. He cited the affidavit of Claire Guthrie Gastañaga, who he described as "probably the most knowledgeable person on academic hiring in the country." She had worked as general counsel to the American Council of Education; she served on the board of the National Association of College and University Attorneys. At Princeton, she had taught sexual harassment law to deans and department heads, and she went on to serve as assistant university counsel and assistant secretary of the corporation at Princeton University. She had worked in the general counsel's office of the University of Virginia. In her affidavit for the Emory case, she argued that Fox-Genovese's record before coming to Emory "raised questions about her ability to be an administrator" and pointed out that the job for which Emory hired her was an administrative one—director of Women's Studies.[26]

What would Emory have found if they had looked harder at her record at the time they were searching for a director of women's studies? McKee said they would have found Sara Elbert, a faculty colleague at Binghamton, who said in her sworn affidavit that Fox-Genovese intentionally inflicted emotional distress on students. And that she "came over to my house. And slipped her hands up my dress. To smooth my pantyhose out." They would have found Professor Bonnie Smith of Rutgers, who also provided an affidavit about Fox-Genovese's intentional infliction of emotional distress on students at Rochester.[27]

Finally McKee turned to the claim of "negligent retention": that Emory knew of Fox-Genovese's misconduct, but nevertheless retained her as Director of Women's Studies. The evidence here came from Pat Michelson, former director of Women's Studies; before Gould started working in that office, Michelson sent a memo referring to the complaints about Fox-Genovese to all students in the program. The memo said, "I have become increasingly distressed this year by the number and kinds of grievances I hear regarding women's studies. It seems the basic procedures designed to ensure that all students are treated fairly are just not working." That meant, McKee said, that "Emory was on notice" about Fox-Genovese's misconduct before Virginia Gould went to work as her assistant.[28]

All that was a preview of what the jury—and the media—would hear at a trial.

The next time the lawyers appeared in court came almost a year later. This time the jury had been selected and was waiting for opening arguments, and the TV crew from the CBS News show *48 Hours* was posted outside. The attorneys met in closed session in the judge's chambers. Four hours later, they emerged and the judge announced that the two sides had settled. Instead of the court airing testimony from the plaintiff's witnesses, Emory would pay—reportedly a million dollars—for the conduct of Elizabeth Fox-Genovese.

But Emory never held disciplinary proceedings to determine whether Fox-Genovese violated university rules about abusive and discriminatory treatment of staff and students. Emory has disciplined other faculty members for abusive conduct—David Garrow, Presidential Distinguished Professor of law at Emory and Pulitzer Prize–winning biographer of Martin Luther King, was suspended for six months without pay in 2003 as punishment for what the press described as an "altercation with a law school employee" that resulted in a misdemeanor charge of simple battery. In that instance, despite the fact that the local court adjudicated the case, Emory officials emphasized to the news media that "the university is following its own internal procedures to review the matter."[29]

Garrow's accuser was Gloria Mann, the law school's director of operations, who said Garrow had "yelled at her and grabbed her by the wrists during a confrontation about noisy construction work."[30]

Garrow denied Mann's allegations. Mann also sued Garrow in the same DeKalb County court where the Fox-Genovese charges were aired, charging him with assault and battery, emotional distress, false imprisonment, and defamation.[31]

The procedure at Emory in the Garrow case consisted of the establishment of a three-member committee of law professors—Garrow is a law professor—appointed by the law school dean and charged with reviewing the incident. The committee interviewed witnesses and reported their findings to the dean, who made the decision to suspend Garrow. The chair of the investigating committee, law professor William Carney, refused to discuss the case with inquiring news people, telling them it was "a confidential personnel matter." However, according to the *Atlanta Journal-Constitution,* "he released a statement that said Garrow's attorney had instructed the professor not to meet with the committee." That attorney, Keegan Federal, told that paper that Garrow would appeal the suspension and "might sue the university."[32] (He did not.) The story of Emory suspending the Pulitzer Prize–winning King biographer made national news—historians around the country, as well as the King family, were asked to comment for the media.[33]

Why didn't Emory establish its own disciplinary proceedings concerning Fox-Genovese, as it did with Garrow? The evidence against her may not have been completely accurate, but it offered a prima facie case for Emory to investigate her conduct. I asked Emory Vice President for Equal Opportunity Programs Robert Ethridge, but he did not respond. I asked Emory's official spokesperson, Jan Gleason, vice president of communications, who had commented for the media on the Garrow case, but on Fox-Genovese she had no comment.

Various faculty members were willing to offer speculations—because Gould had sued Emory as well as Fox-Genovese, Emory considered itself to be "on the same side" as Fox-Genovese—but they provided nothing authoritative.

While Emory did nothing to consider whether Fox-Genovese had violated university rules, she solidified her position as a conservative hero who stood up to the feminists. The *Chronicle of Higher Education*, which always has its finger on the pulse of controversy in academia, ran a couple of key pieces about Fox-Genovese the year before she won her White House award. One argued that the women's movement had "summarily shunned" her because she rejected the "feminist party line," because she challenged "political correctness."[34] Another opinion piece in the *Chronicle* praised her as a "leading neoconservative critic of women's studies" who belonged on the list of America's top 100 public intellectuals.[35] The same year the right-wing *Washington Times* praised Fox-Genovese's writing.[36]

For the conservative media, Fox-Genovese was not only a woman who stood up to feminist political correctness at Emory; she also took on "the feminists" in the book published the same year that her court case came to trial. The title said it all: *Feminism Is Not the Story of My Life.* The book argued—repeatedly—that feminists are elitists: "elite" professionals who treat their secretaries badly, "elite" careerists who don't understand the lives of their female underlings, "elite" achievers in designer suits who have no sympathy for,

or interest in, the "average" woman. The indictment has an un-
canny similarity to the charges made against Fox-Genovese herself
by female underlings at Emory. As Susan Faludi wrote in reviewing
the book for *The Nation,* "Who's calling whom elitist?"[37]

The book received passionate denunciations from feminist reviewers, who criticized Fox-Genovese for failing to fulfill her prom-
ise to explore the experiences of real women, and for presenting a
stereotyped and false description of feminism. Mary Gordon reviewed the book for the *New York Times Book Review.* She opened by
recalling that, in Fox-Genovese's previous book, *Feminism Without
Illusions*, she ended by criticizing people who "find it easy to blame
feminism for some of the most disturbing aspects of modern life:
divorce, latchkey children, teen-age alcoholism, domestic violence,
the sexual abuse of children." Five years later, Gordon wrote, "it
seems she has become one of the people she warned us about." She
described the book as "not really a sustained argument but a series of
pronouncements reeled off at a manic pace. Ms. Fox-Genovese
strives for aphoristic trenchancy, but La Rochefoucauld she is not."[38]
Ruth Conniff in the *Progressive* described the book as "another install-
ment in the seemingly endless anti-feminist saga," and asked, "Is
there no limit to the amount of media attention and grant money
women authors who declare war on the women's movement can at-
tract?"[39]

The fierceness of the criticisms coming from the left of course only
increased Fox-Genovese's standing on the right as a brave and committed fighter. She won high praise in the key right-wing venues
Commentary, the *Washington Times,* and the *Weekly Standard*, which

helped pave the way for her White House award.[40] After Bush paid tribute to her in a White House ceremony, the *Weekly Standard* congratulated her: "Well done, and well deserved."[41]

The case of Elizabeth Fox-Genovese shows that some kinds of misconduct by some people—in this case, abusive treatment of staff and students—are not thought to merit disciplinary action within academia. It shows they can be spun into political capital by friendly media—which, at least for historians on the right, can help earn big rewards in Republican Washington, D.C.

2

The Alger Hiss Case, the Archives, and Allen Weinstein

*G*o ahead, try. Name the archivist of the United States. It's a pretty fair bet you failed. The archivist—at this writing, former Kansas governor John Carlin—has traditionally been one of the lower profile jobs in the federal hierarchy, but, as its website notes, the National Archives is not simply "a dusty hoard of ancient history. It is a public trust on which our democracy depends. It enables people to inspect for themselves the record of what government has done."[1]

That's why the White House nomination in April 2004 of a new archivist—Allen Weinstein, a historian of Soviet espionage—was greeted by a storm of protest in the normally quiet world of archivists and historians. Almost two dozen organizations including the American Historical Association, the Society of American

Archivists, and the Organization of American Historians issued a joint statement expressing concern and calling on the Senate, which has to confirm such nominations, to hold hearings to find out why the current archivist was being replaced and whether Weinstein was qualified for the position.[2]

The historians and archivists objected first because the nomination was clearly a political move, while the position of archivist was supposed to have been depoliticized. Weinstein had close ties to Republicans in Congress, and the board of his Center for Democracy included Republican senators Kay Bailey Hutchinson and Richard Lugar, House Republican Whip Roy Blunt, and Henry Kissinger. The archivist should be a nonpolitical appointment, because as the custodian of the nation's history, he is confronted with issues that have major political consequences—from the JFK assassination records to the Nixon White House tapes—and the decisions about access ought to be nonpartisan. This is why the archivist's term is not linked to the president's. It is indefinite. He can serve forever and can be fired by the president only for cause.

There was no need to replace the archivist who was in office—John Carlin, a Clinton appointee—at that point; he had made it clear he intended to remain at his post until July 2005. Carlin did announce early in April 2004, that he would leave before that—reportedly in response to White House pressure—but declared in his statement that he was not resigning until his successor was sworn in.[3]

Why then did the White House nominate a new archivist? Many speculated that the president, as well as his father, thought he might lose the election, and they wanted their man in control of their archives before that happened. The new archivist was scheduled to deal with a number of major issues, starting with access to the archives of the 9-11 Commission after it closed up shop in August 2004. He was also expected to deal with the release of the archives of the presidency of Bush Senior, which, under the Presidential Records Act, could have been made public starting in 2005 (except, of course, for classified documents). These records included, for example, documents on Bush Senior's role in the Iran-Contra scandal of the late 1980s, when he was Reagan's vice president. And the president and his father may have been concerned also that, if Bush Junior lost the election, the new archivist would have a third new task: appointing a director for the Bush Junior presidential archives.

Whatever Bush's motives may have been, Allen Weinstein was considered by many archivists and historians to have been unqualified on ethical grounds. They pointed to his buying exclusive access to restricted archives for his 1999 book on Soviet espionage, *The Haunted Wood,* and his withholding of archival materials from other scholars, which appear to violate the ethical standards of the archivists' and historians' organizations.

First, buying exclusive access: for his 1999 book, *The Haunted Wood: Soviet Espionage in America—The Stalin Era,* Weinstein's publisher Random House in 1992 paid a group of retired KGB agents a substantial amount of money—he's told people $100,000—in exchange for "exclusive" access to the KGB archives. This appears to violate the code of ethics of the International Council on Archivists, which calls for "the widest possible access" to documents.[4] It's wrong for a historian to pay archivists not to provide information to others. It prevents others from checking the accuracy and completeness of his work.

Other historians with other publishers did it the right way: when Yale University Press obtained access to the Moscow archives of the Communist Party, editors pledged to make their documents available to other researchers. Jonathan Brent, now editorial director of the Annals of Communism book series at Yale, explained in the *New York Times* that they made that pledge because "we want to enhance scholarship, not impede it."[5]

Commercial publishers of course want exclusive access in order to make a profit, but the archivist of the U.S. should be held to a higher standard. Joyce Appleby, past president of the American Historical Association and emeritus professor of history at UCLA, told me, "Buying exclusive access raises serious ethical questions." Ellen Schrecker, a leading historian of McCarthyism, also pointed to "the ethical questions that buying exclusive access to official archives raises."[6]

Brent added that "KGB files are very problematic from the standpoint of authenticity and reliability," which makes it all the more important for other scholars to see the materials Weinstein used in his research. But the Russian government withdrew access to the KGB archives. Amy Knight, a scholar of Soviet history, wrote in the *Wilson Quarterly* about the consequences of this problem for Weinstein's book: "Many of the standards by which scholars traditionally judge historical writings have been lowered, or discarded altogether" in works like *The Haunted Wood,* which rely on unverified information purporting to come from KGB files.[7]

Similar objections to the new Weinstein book were raised by Anna K. Nelson, a distinguished adjunct historian in residence at the American University with extensive experience in governmental archives policy; she was partly responsible for the Presidential Records Act protecting the Nixon White House documents, and she was a member of the John F. Kennedy Assassination Records Review Board. She has testified before Congress, representing the American Historical Association, the Organization of American Historians, and the Society of American Archivists. Writing about *The Haunted Wood* in the *Chronicle of Higher Education,* Nelson pointed out the basic problem in Weinstein's work: the "special access given to Weinstein" was "problematical": "Many questions could be answered if other scholars could examine the same records. But Russian officials have now closed the K.G.B. files to researchers, and we have no way to confirm the contents of this book."[8]

Weinstein has also been charged with other improprieties and misrepresentations in *The Haunted Wood*—charges that come from an unlikely source: his co-author Alexander Vassiliev. In the course of a 2003 trial in London, Vassiliev complained, as he had done earlier, that Weinstein among other derelictions had never shown him the manuscript before it was published. If true, that is clearly improper. Weinstein doesn't read Russian—the deal with the former KGB agents permitted Vassiliev to take notes on documents from the archives, selected by former KGB officers, and Vassiliev gave notes in English to Weinstein. Thus Weinstein has never seen the documents on which his book is based. This is a problem because Vassiliev has told at least one interviewer—Susan Butler, biographer of Amelia Earhart—that he disagreed with some of Weinstein's claims about KGB documents that appear in the book.[9] If Vassiliev is right that Weinstein has misrepresented the documents, that should disqualify him from the archivist position.

A related problem concerns Weinstein's documentation of his sources in *The Haunted Wood.* On this point he has been criticized by people who agree with his conclusions. Sam Tanenhaus, now editor of the *New York Times Book Review* and author of the leading biography of Whittaker Chambers, criticized *The Haunted Wood* in the *New Republic,* where Weinstein has often published. Tanenhaus wrote that he agreed with Weinstein about Hiss and Chambers, but that *The Haunted Wood* was marred by what he called Weinstein's "failure" to document his sources properly. He did not use the accepted system of referencing these archival documents—the result, Tanenhaus wrote, of the fact that Weinstein has "a weakness for mystification"—not a quality you want in the archivist of the United States.[10]

The second major ethical problem in Weinstein's work is his politically motivated withholding of documents. Weinstein's book *Perjury,* published in 1978, presented new evidence that Alger Hiss, the prominent New Deal figure accused of espionage in 1947 by former Communist Whittaker Chambers, was guilty as charged; most reviewers said Weinstein's new evidence had laid the case to rest. Weinstein's research was challenged, however, by Victor Navasky, editor of *The Nation,* who contacted six of Weinstein's key sources and found that each of them said he or she had been misquoted or otherwise misrepresented in the book.[11]

Weinstein replied that his interviewees were recanting after seeing conclusions with which they disagreed and that he had tape recordings of his interviews to prove he had quoted them correctly.

He invited Navasky to hear the tapes; Navasky accepted. But when Navasky arrived at Weinstein's home at the agreed-upon time, Weinstein refused to let him hear the tapes.[12] Weinstein then stated in the *New Republic,* "All my files and tapes will be available to Victor Navasky and everyone else at the Truman Library later this year."[13] That was 1978.

Twenty-five years later, Weinstein has never deposited the tapes at the Truman Library or any other archive. Weinstein's refusal to make the disputed materials available to other scholars today violates the AHA "Statement on Standards of Professional Conduct" adopted in 1987: historians should "make available to others their sources, evidence, and data, including the documentation they develop through interviews." The AHA statement requires "free, open, equal, and nondiscriminatory access" to sources.[14] Weinstein also is not complying with the 1989 AHA "Statement on Interviewing for Historical Documentation," developed jointly with the Oral History Association, the Organization of American Historians, and the Society of American Archivists; it declares that "interviewers should arrange to deposit their interviews in an archival repository that is capable of . . . making them available for general research."[15]

The Hiss case constitutes a pivotal event in the history of the cold war and the rise of McCarthyism. Hiss's conviction for perjury (the statute of limitations had run out on espionage) transformed public opinion, persuading Americans that domestic Communism posed a real danger to the country; the case helped convince Americans of the validity of Republican charges that the Democrats were soft on communism. The obscure congressman from Southern

California who pushed the case became a senator, then vice president, and eventually president; the House Un-American Activities Committee (HUAC) gained credibility and power and spent the next two decades hunting Reds; a month after Hiss's conviction, Senator Joseph McCarthy made his famous speech in Wheeling, West Virginia, launching himself into the center of American politics and giving the new, virulent anti-Communist politics its name.[16]

During the initial HUAC investigations, Chambers charged Hiss with Communist Party membership but denied for four months that they had engaged in espionage. He accused Hiss of espionage only after Hiss sued him for libel. At the time, Hiss had impeccable liberal credentials: he was president of the Carnegie Foundation and had been a New Deal State Department high official, serving on FDR's staff at the Yalta conference. Initially the FBI, the Justice Department, and the House Un-American Activities Committee believed Hiss's denials. Chambers won the support of only one member of HUAC—a first-term congressman from Southern California named Richard Nixon.

In a historic media event, Chambers led HUAC investigators in 1948 to a pumpkin patch in Westminster, Maryland, opened a hollowed-out pumpkin, and pulled out microfilm he said included copies of secret State Department documents Hiss had given him in 1938, when Hiss was a State Department official, to transmit to the Soviets. (Chambers's pumpkin patch was declared a National Historical Monument by the Reagan administration, and a reproduction of the pumpkin is displayed in the Nixon Library in Yorba Linda, California. The National Park Service advisory board had opposed the designation, arguing that historians needed more time for "an objective assessment" of the significance of the site.)[17]

Weinstein's new evidence was vital to the Hiss-Chambers case because at the time of Hiss's two trials, in 1950, the government prosecutors had little corroborating evidence to support Chambers's accusations; the evidence against Hiss was Chambers's testimony, and the jury had to decide which man was telling the truth. The first trial resulted in a hung jury; the second jury believed Chambers. During the four-month interval between the trials, the Soviets detonated their first atom bomb, and the Communists won power in China, intensifying cold war hysteria in the U.S. over Communist espionage. The fact that Hiss was convicted in this overheated atmosphere created a cloud of doubt about the verdict that did not dissipate during the next three decades.

Weinstein's new evidence was significant because it seemed to resolve those doubts. Although he produced no new interviewees that directly implicated Hiss, he did present interviews corroborating Chambers's statements on other matters; these made the book historically significant. *Time* magazine published an excerpt from the book, and the *New York Review of Books* and the *New Republic* published Weinstein's statements defending his work, along with strongly positive reviews of the book, when it appeared.[18] George Will wrote in *Newsweek* that the book was a "historic event . . . stunningly meticulous and a monument to the intellectual ideal of truth stalked to its hiding place."[19] Alfred Kazin wrote in *Esquire,* "After this book, it is impossible to imagine anything new in this case except an admission by Alger Hiss that he has been lying for thirty years."[20]

Then Victor Navasky came along with something that was new. Navasky's method was simple, although no other reviewer undertook it: he located six key interviewees, mailed them copies of the pages in the book that referred to them, and asked whether they had been quoted correctly and in context. All six replied that they had been misquoted, misrepresented, or misconstrued—an extraordinary result. Ella Winter was one of Weinstein's key new sources; she had been Lincoln Steffens's wife during the 1930s. Weinstein quoted her as saying Chambers had "previously tried—and failed— to recruit her for the underground," and that she "corroborated Chambers's role as an underground courier."[21] But Winter told Navasky that "Chambers never tried to recruit me for underground work or even for the CP" and that "I never had any idea that 'Chambers' was an underground courier."[22]

Maxim Lieber, another key source of Weinstein's, was described in the book as Chambers's "sometime associate in the underground," who "identified Peters as 'the head of the whole Communist espionage apparatus in this country.'" According to Weinstein, Lieber said "some things are romanticized in [Whittaker Chambers's book] *Witness,* but most of it—as I know of the incidents—is true."[23] But Lieber told Navasky that Weinstein "made all these things up of whole cloth. . . . I could not have identified Peters as head of the underground because I knew nothing about the underground. . . . I never read *Witness.*"[24]

Paul Willert, American head of Oxford Press, according to Weinstein was "himself engaged in 'secret work' for the underground German Communist Party earlier in the 1930s . . . and he maintained close connections with the American Communist Party in

1938." According to Weinstein, he "confirmed the essential elements in Chambers's account of their relationship."[25] But Willert told Navasky, "Weinstein's book and Weinstein's references are inaccurate, untrue, or half truths." He denied being a member of the Communist Party.[26]

Sam Krieger was another of Weinstein's key sources. Weinstein described Krieger as a sinister and notorious figure, "an important Communist organizer during the Gastonia textile strike of 1929" who "fled to the Soviet Union . . . after being jailed by local authorities," and then returned to recruit Chambers.[27] Krieger said these were falsehoods; he had been a lowly Party person working as circulation manager of the Yonkers *Statesman*; Weinstein had confused him with another man who used the same Party alias. Alden Whitman and Karel Kaplan also told Navasky they had been misquoted or misrepresented. Navasky concluded that "*Perjury* settles nothing about the Hiss case. . . . Whatever new data Weinstein may have gathered are fatally tainted by his unprofessionalism."[28]

The disputed quotes did not by themselves prove or disprove the guilt of Alger Hiss. Garry Wills, who wrote a strongly positive review of the book for the *New York Review of Books,* told me in an interview, "I was not convinced of Hiss's guilt by the quotes from Weinstein's interviews; I was convinced by other things, including my own talk with people who knew Hiss and my talk with Hiss himself."[29] But Weinstein's disputed interviews all concerned the issue of Chambers's credibility—the central issue in the case. All the new sources were marshaled by Weinstein to show that Chambers was a truthful man. Weinstein himself claimed that "the most important kind of verification" for his thesis was this new "corroboration" for

Chambers's story.[30] But if the new sources were misquoted or misrepresented, the book's thesis would be damaged, and the claim that it definitively resolved the case would be undermined. Moreover, any author who misquoted or misconstrued six out of six sources would find his research and conclusions judged inadequate and unconvincing, if not fraudulent.

Weinstein understood the seriousness of the evidence against him. He wrote in the *New Republic* that Navasky had made "grave accusations against a scholar," but declared, "I have cited all six accurately. Three of the six interviewees who recanted their stories—Maxim Lieber, Karel Kaplan, and Sam Krieger—are on tape. . . . In all six cases—these three plus Paul Willert, Ella Winter, and Alden Whitman—I have not only the notes of my interviews but also letters from them, defense file memos, FBI records and other interviews that corroborate their statements." Lieber's statements to Navasky were "outright falsehoods, discredited by a mass of material, including his own words in a tape-recorded interview and by letters he wrote to me in 1976. Lieber told me—I have it on tape—that he had worked on occasional underground assignments when ordered by J. Peters to engage in these." Weinstein also wrote, "In my interview with Ella Winter in 1975, she described in detail Chambers's efforts to recruit her."[31]

Navasky should have contacted him before publishing his critique, Weinstein wrote. Navasky replied that he rejected the argument that "because I bothered to check out his sources, I was somehow obliged—unlike other reviewers—to get in touch with him. . . . If the book's sources can't survive a minimal fact-checking then no amount of ex parte communications from the author can save it."[32] Weinstein repeated the invitation in the *Washington Post,* which reported that he "invites Navasky, Hiss or anybody else to examine his thousands of documents, his tapes and notes, his original 1,600 page manuscript."[33]

Navasky took up the invitation, and reported that Weinstein "invited us to inspect his files. . . . 'To prevent a "fishing expedition" in my 50,000 page archive' he asked me to specify in advance the list of items I wished to see. . . . We limited our request to 20 items." At the agreed-upon time, Navasky and two associates arrived at Weinstein's door. "We were met by Mrs. Weinstein who told us that her husband had changed his mind and that we would not be allowed to inspect the files."[34]

In response, Weinstein explained in the *New Republic* that "I have been inundated with requests from scholars and others for access to these materials, and have decided this is the best way to provide it without totally disrupting my life and other work." Then he pledged that "all my files and tapes" would be "available" at the Truman Library "later this year"—that was 1978.[35]

In the meantime, Sam Krieger sued Weinstein, his publisher Alfred A. Knopf, and the *New Republic* for libel.[36] Weinstein had written in the magazine about Krieger, "He too is on tape, and his words are also quoted verbatim."[37] During discovery proceedings, Weinstein failed to produce the tape of his interview with Krieger. The magazine published a retraction, in which Weinstein declared that his "statements about Sam Krieger were erroneous."[38] Weinstein, Knopf, and the magazine paid a "substantial five-figure sum" to Krieger, *New York* magazine reported, in settlement of the libel case.[39]

The controversy reached the pages of the *New York Times,* which published half a dozen articles about Weinstein's book and Navasky's critique; it was covered also by *Newsweek,* the *Washington Post,* and the *Today Show.* Navasky's critique led at least one of the reviewers of the book to change his positive evaluation of it: Christopher Lehmann-Haupt wrote in the *New York Times,* "Instead of finally settling an ideological battle that has been fought intermittently for 30 years now *Perjury* appears to be just another incident in the war."[40]

In a telephone interview in 1991, Weinstein, by then president of the Center for Democracy in Washington, D.C., told me that he did not donate the tapes to the Truman Library because "there was an organized campaign that required me to defend myself against litigation that related to those files; on the advice of counsel at the time it made no sense to make those files handy." This advice from counsel was not a vote of confidence in the accuracy of Weinstein's scholarship, and it contradicted the AHA Standards of Professional Conduct. "At this distance in time," he continued in our 1991 interview, "I'm happy to say that I'm happy to consider any request from any scholar for specific files they would like to look at." But to "consider" requests from other scholars for access is very different from what the AHA Standards of Professional Conduct require: providing "free, open, equal, and nondiscriminatory access" to sources, and depositing the interviews "in an archival repository that is capable of . . . making them available for general research."

Weinstein gave the impression that scholars who shared his interpretation would be given access, while those who disagreed with him would not. He denied that this was the case: "Every scholar that has asked me for materials in last seven or eight years, who has moved fairly far along in their own research, has had access to what they wanted. This includes foreign scholars. I remember a professor from Oslo who wanted to see my Cantwell files. There have been a bunch of Chambers biographers as well." I asked him for names. He promised to "dig up the names of people who have had access to my papers," but he never me sent any names.

William Reuben, a longtime Hiss defender who has been working for many years on a biography of Chambers, requested access to the disputed files, but Weinstein refused: "I asked him at the OAH convention in Reno in 1988," Reuben told me. "He said he would get back to me after the weekend; he never did."[41]

In our interview, Weinstein stated, "The process of interviewing for my book was the same for any book for which live subjects are available; I know of few scholars who have donated interview materials. Do you?" Ronald Grele, at the time director of Columbia University Oral History Archive, told me, "Many people have donated interviews to us; it's a regular practice here. We get them all the time. Other oral history projects do the same thing. We have twenty or thirty collections that were donated. Recent donations came from Ellen Schrecker, who donated her tapes for *No Ivory Tower;* Eric Barnouw, who donated his tapes for his history of radio; and Linda Fasulo, who donated forty interviews for her book about U.N. diplomats. We've been given over 300 hours done for the new book *Addicts Who Survived*—the authors note in their book that we have their interviews so that other scholars will be able to use them."[42]

In his interview with me, Weinstein went on to say, "I'm happy to donate all the material to the Truman Library; the question is under what conditions." The AHA statement clearly states the conditions: "free, open, equal, and nondiscriminatory access." Truman Library archivist Dennis Bilger told me that Weinstein had not returned their calls for several years: "When we try to contact him at the Center for Democracy in Washington, our experience over the last several years is that he isn't available. You talk to one secretary, you talk to another secretary, but you never get to talk to him. One time he returned a call of mine, but it was early in the morning, before we opened, and he left a message with the guard. That's one of the few times we've had contact with him. Basically we've gotten tired of trying to contact him and haven't tried in over a year."[43]

Weinstein did send some materials to the Truman Archive, but they were not the disputed interview tapes. "We have some papers of Weinstein's here," archivist Dennis Bilger said, "but what we have isn't worth much—primarily Xerox copies of FBI files, stuff that's available to anyone who goes to the FBI in Washington. The copies are very poor quality, difficult to read. A person doing serious research would do better to work at the FBI in Washington. Weinstein also gave us some correspondence of his with the ACLU regarding his suit against the FBI. He promised to give us tape recordings of interviews used in his book *Perjury,* but he never did. We never got any tapes, and we never got any deed of gift for the papers he did give us. We've asked him numerous times to sign a deed of gift for the papers he did give us, but he hasn't done so. In our view, we have physical custody of the papers he sent and are providing courtesy storage for them." When I asked Weinstein why he hadn't signed a deed of gift for the papers, he replied, "Bilger should call and visit the next time he's in Washington."

Bilger provided an update in 2003: "Professor Weinstein has signed a deed of gift for his papers; however, no additional papers have come to the Library since 1992. . . . Almost all of the Weinstein 'papers' consist of copies of FBI documents with the rest dealing with correspondence with the ACLU regarding Weinstein's FOI suit against the FBI to get this material released. In short, there is no change in the status of the Weinstein papers other than the fact that he finally did sign the deed of gift. I am not sure of the status of the tape recordings except that he did not send copies to the Truman Library. Without these tapes, there is not much original material here that would not be in the FBI files in Washington, D.C."[44]

The conclusion seems inescapable: Weinstein's refusal to make available to other scholars the disputed interviews for his book on the Hiss case violates AHA guidelines and professional standards. The fact that he repeatedly promised to do so compounds the offense. His offer to "consider" requests for access does not satisfy the AHA requirements of "free, open, equal, and nondiscriminatory access." The interviews provide vital evidence about a central event in the history of the cold war, which makes scholarly access to them more important. And the fact that his interviewees have challenged the accuracy of Weinstein's scholarship, and that the tapes can resolve a longstanding controversy about Weinstein's book, makes release of them essential. The materials may confirm Weinstein's claim that his disputed interviews were accurate and in context; as

Garry Wills wrote in 1978, "People you interview often want to change their story once they see how you've juxtaposed it with other information."[45] Making the tapes available would resolve that issue. Garry Wills, who believes Hiss was guilty, told me, "Weinstein said he would donate the tapes; clearly he should do it."[46]

What do you do when you come up against this kind of case of scholarly wrongdoing? You can complain to scholarly associations such as the American Historical Association (AHA), which takes the responsibility for stating the profession's ethical standards and enforcing them. In 1990, the AHA published a twenty-seven-page "Statement on Standards of Professional Conduct," covering matters such as plagiarism, fair practices in recruitment, and sexual harassment. The "Statement on Standards" begins with a lofty call on historians to "become more cognizant of their professional responsibilities." But try and write for AHA publications about particular cases of violations of the statement on standards. I did. I met with obstructions, delays, and diversions; the professional association seemed strangely reluctant to enforce its own ethical standards.

In September 1990, I submitted to the AHA newsletter *Perspectives* (circulation 15,000) an article about Allen Weinstein's book *Perjury* and his refusal to make his interviews available to other researchers, as required by the statement on standards. Here was a case in which a scholar was clearly violating a strongly stated principle of the history profession. But when I tried to bring the Weinstein case into the pages of the AHA newsletter, officials expressed reluctance even to permit public discussion of the organization's statement on standards. AHA officials formally advised me to delete references to their statement on ethics in the article I had submitted to them for publication. This sad story tells much about the professional associations' strange anxiety about scrutinizing scholarly ethics.

In my submission I quoted the AHA "Statement on Standards," which states on its very first page that historians should "make available to others their sources, evidence, and data, including the documentation they develop through interviews." I quoted the second page, which says this access must be "free, open, equal, and nondiscriminatory." I quoted the AHA "Statement on Interviewing for Historical Documentation," which declares that "interviewers should arrange to deposit their interviews in an archival repository that is capable of . . . making them available for general research." The manuscript I submitted to the AHA concluded by urging Weinstein to fulfill his own promises as well as the ethical requirements of the profession and make his materials available to other scholars.

AHA Newsletter Editor Kathy Koziara-Herbert accepted my article for publication in the newsletter's "Archives and Research" column, scheduled it for the December 1990 issue, and faxed a copy of the manuscript to Weinstein in September, telling him the AHA newsletter editors "would very much welcome a reply from you to an article we intend to publish." The November issue of the newsletter announced the article as forthcoming on its front page: "Coming up in Future Issues: . . . Will the Weinstein tapes of the Hiss case ever be available to researchers? Jon Wiener reexamines this question in 'The Alger Hiss Case, the Archives, and Allen Weinstein.'"

But the article was not published as scheduled. The AHA executive director at the time, Samuel R. Gammon, overruled the decision of the newsletter editors and blocked its publication. AHA Deputy Executive Director James B. Gardner wrote to me in December 1990, "We cannot publish your charges against Allen Weinstein without first conducting a thorough investigation." The proper investigative body, he said, was the AHA's Professional Division, the six-member elected body established in 1974 and charged with enforcing the profession's code of ethics.

Gardner had a suggestion: my article should be turned into a complaint, and submitted to the Professional Division for adjudication. That would keep it out of print, because the AHA did not publish complaints, and the Professional Division kept its proceedings secret. Once a year, the division published a report on its activities; it spoke only in vague generalities and never mentioned any names. Turning my 2,500-word article into a complaint would bury it forever, so I rejected that suggestion.

If I continued to seek publication, I was informed, my article would not only be investigated by the six-member Professional Division, it would also have to be "reviewed" by the thirteen-member Council of the AHA—the organization's governing body. This for a 2,500-word article which had already been reviewed and accepted by two newsletter editors. It's unlikely that any other article at the AHA aroused more pre-publication editorial anxiety. No one I talked to had ever heard of the AHA executive director blocking publication of an article accepted for publication by the association's editors. One newsletter editor suggested that Weinstein, instead of replying in print to the criticism, may have contacted Executive Director

Gammon privately and issued some kind of threat—perhaps of a libel suit. When I asked Gardner whether this could have happened, he did not reply.

In view of the seeming impropriety of the executive director interfering with the editorial decisions at the newsletter, I filed a complaint against him with the Professional Division in February 1991, asking the division to rule that, since the article "fulfilled all the requirements of normal scholarship—it cited its sources fully—the editors' judgment that it merited publication should be reaffirmed." The alternative—an "investigation"—seemed unnecessary. What was there to investigate? As I wrote, "Any questions about the accuracy of my article could have been easily answered by quickly checking the sources cited in the notes"—an action that should have been the responsibility of the newsletter editors, not the distinguished members of the Professional Division or the council. And since Weinstein had been already offered the opportunity to reply in print, he had been given the chance to correct any errors.

The larger issue concerned the proper forum for arguments about ethical violations. My criticism of Weinstein belonged in the public arena; it was part of the world of scholarly exchange and debate. The AHA Professional Division, I argued, instead of seeking to adjudicate disputes of this type in secret, should encourage the widest possible discussion of ethical issues among the profession and the interested public. The intellectual life of the history profession lies in published debate, not in the confidential adjudication of secret complaints by the Professional Division. So I argued in my letter.

That was February 1991. In mid-May I got the Professional Division's reply, written by Chair Susan Socolow of Emory University:

my argument was rejected. In blocking publication of my article, the AHA officials "acted appropriately." But nothing in the letter indicated that the division had fulfilled its assignment of "conducting a thorough investigation" of my "charges." Instead, the division established conditions under which it would "consider publication of a revised manuscript": first, my article could not appear in the "Archives" section, where the editors had put it; it could appear only in the "Viewpoints" section.

The second condition was extraordinary: "we ask that you delete or reword references to the Statement on Standards of Professional Conduct in order to make it clear that you are stating a personal opinion." Delete references to the "Statement on Standards"? Didn't they want scholars to write about ethical issues, to give life to these guidelines, to which the AHA had devoted considerable time and effort?

If I complied with these requirements, I was told, my revised manuscript would be reviewed by the Professional Division; Weinstein would be sent a new copy, and given another ninety days in which to respond; then the manuscript and any reply from Weinstein would be submitted to the thirteen-member council for review; if the council approved, the revised article could then be published.

Willing by now to do almost anything to get my article into the newsletter, I accepted all the conditions and submitted a revised article for review by the Professional Division and the AHA Council. I thought readers would understand that, when a piece was headlined "Viewpoint" and signed by the author, it expressed the viewpoint of the author; the AHA, however, feared readers wouldn't get it, and I deferred to their judgment. Thus in the revised piece I chose to "reword" rather than "delete" references to the "Statement on Standards," inserting the phrase "in my opinion" before my statement that Weinstein's actions violated the AHA statement on standards.

The division accepted the revised manuscript and in July sent a copy to Weinstein, asking him to respond within ninety days. We waited eagerly to see what Weinstein would do this time; at the end of three months, he again had failed to reply. The article was then forwarded to the council for its review; they approved publication. "The Alger Hiss Case, the Archives, and Allen Weinstein" finally appeared in the February 1992 issue of *Perspectives,* a year and a half after it had been accepted, a year and two months after it had been originally scheduled to appear.

This occasion should have been a cause for celebration. But between the idea and the reality falls the shadow: the article was preceded by a lengthy and misleading headnote. It explained that "publication was delayed" because "with the concurrence of the Council, the Division agreed to publication on the condition that Mr. Weinstein first be given an opportunity to respond to Mr. Wiener's charges." That was untrue: publication had not been delayed to give Weinstein a chance to reply; the editors of the newsletter had solicited a reply long before publication had been delayed by the director. The reason why publication was delayed, according to Deputy Executive Director Gardner's letter to me, was to permit the division to conduct an "investigation" into the accuracy of my charges. But no statement appeared in the headnote indicating that the accuracy of my charges had been verified by an AHA investigation.

The headnote should have ended, "The manuscript was conveyed to Mr. Weinstein, who chose not to respond." That would have provided a great opening and strong confirmation of the justice of my complaint. Instead, the headnote concluded (after referring to Weinstein's not responding), "The Council reminds readers that publication in *Perspectives* should not be viewed as an alternative to the formal review process overseen by the Professional Division."

The council thus introduced my article to readers with a sort of reprimand for my failing to file a formal complaint. The headnote was consistent with the concerns the Professional Division had expressed in its ruling on my case: they had instructed me to "avoid any impression that the Division has received a formal complaint, reviewed the charges, or reached a finding." Apparently they were still willing to receive a complaint. If publication was not "an alternative to the formal review process," that meant you didn't have to choose between publishing and filing a complaint; you could do both.

Taking heart from this advice, and eager to do the right thing, I filed a formal complaint against Weinstein in February 1992 with the Professional Division, submitting my published article as the text of the complaint, asking them to conclude that Weinstein had violated the "Statement on Standards" and to advise him that he had an ethical responsibility to make his documents available at an archive. Five months later I received a three-sentence reply to my complaint, again from Deputy Executive Director Gardner: the Professional Division "must recuse itself from review of the complaint," he wrote, "since the charges have been made public through publication in the Association's newsletter."

The AHA's policy now seemed to be that the association would not consider an ethical question if the public knew what the question was. The logic behind that policy was hard to follow, but perhaps some principle had eluded me. For enlightenment I turned to the "Addendum on Policies and Procedures" at the end of the "Statement on Standards," but in that section there was no requirement that the Professional Division "recuse itself" from cases of which the public was aware.

Gardner's letter concluded that the division "does not see that any purpose will be served by further action on this matter." I could see some: the argument that Weinstein ought to fulfill his ethical responsibilities could be more than the opinion of one person—it could be the formal judgment of the profession's highest body. If that happened, the profession's ethical standards would have been given life by the AHA, scholars would have been reminded by the AHA's action of their obligations to each other, and maybe even Weinstein would comply, providing other historians of the cold war era with valuable primary source materials.

Weinstein published an updated version of *Perjury* in 1997, which contained a "Note on Documentation": "When *Perjury*'s original edition was published in 1978, my intention was to deposit the 60,000 pages of material used in preparing the book at the Harry S. Truman Library. A lawsuit apparently encouraged by supporters of Alger Hiss against the author, his publisher, and *The New Republic* magazine—subsequently settled without trial—made it advisable to maintain the files accumulated through personal research. . . . Also, various scholars, including Sam Tanenhaus, recent biographer of Whittaker Chambers, have made extensive use of my personal research files with permission."[47]

Yes, the lawsuit was settled out of court. But, as Victor Navasky pointed out in *The Nation,* "that was because Weinstein and Co. agreed to corrections and apologies" and, according to *New York* magazine, a payment to one of the misquoted interviewees of $17,500. Tanenhaus of course agreed with Weinstein about Hiss and never questioned his problematic sources. "It's nice to know that, unlike those who disagreed with Weinstein's findings, Tanenhaus had access to his files," Navasky wrote. "But neither Weinstein nor Tanenhaus had the scholarly integrity to deal with the protests of those interviewees who didn't take him to court."[48] (Later Tanenhaus would criticize *The Haunted Wood,* as noted on page thirty-six.)

That's the "Note on Documentation" in the new edition of *Perjury.* As for the text, in the new edition Weinstein simply reprinted the disputed interviews without indicating that they had been disputed or providing any additional documentation to establish their accuracy.

And there were new problems in the new edition. According to the publisher's press release, the new edition incorporated "recently released critical evidence from the KGB archives opened *exclusively* to the author" (emphasis mine).[49] Once again Weinstein was making his argument on the basis of evidence available to no one else.

But Weinstein has suffered little professional stigma because of his violations of professional standards and the questions raised about his research. At the time his book *Perjury* was first published, he was a professor of history at Smith College and chair of its American Studies program. He left Smith in 1981 to become University

Professor at Georgetown University. In 1985, he was named University Professor and Professor of History at Boston University. After that, he described himself as "founder, President and CEO of The Center for Democracy." His bio lists many awards and honors.[50] In recent years, he's reviewed for the *Washington Post* and the *Los Angeles Times*.[51] *Perjury* continues to be cited as a major if not definitive study.

Whatever one thinks of Weinstein's conclusions about Soviet espionage, his methods of dealing with archives have been problematic from an ethical standpoint. Why then was Weinstein able to get away with violating the historians' code of scholarly ethics—and win a White House nomination to be archivist of the U.S.? He's on the popular side of an old debate; he defended the conventional wisdom about Alger Hiss. The people who have questioned the book's documentation did not have the power to get their case into the mainstream—partly because the mainstream really doesn't want to have to deal with the possibility that something is seriously wrong with the leading work claiming to prove the guilt of Alger Hiss.

Conservative pundits at the *Weekly Standard* and the *National Review* often claim the left controls the history profession.[52] But with Allen Weinstein, the right demonstrated far more power to reward its historians—with White House nominations.

For an update on Weinstein's nomination, please turn to page 215.

3

Facing Black Students at Harvard: Stephan Thernstrom Takes a Stand

When the Bush White House nominated Harvard historian Stephan Thernstrom to a term on the National Council on the Humanities in 2002, the *Harvard Crimson* described him as "a conservative."[1] But Thernstrom wasn't just any conservative historian; he had made page one of the *Crimson* a decade earlier when he was the target of black student complaints about one of his lectures, and his defiant response had made him a neocon hero. The *Crimson* had forgotten about this, but the Republican establishment remembered.

Thernstrom gained prominence in Republican circles for the books he wrote with his wife Abigail criticizing affirmative action. In *America in Black and White,* published in 1997, and in their 2003 book *No Excuses: Closing the Racial Gap in Learning America,* the

Thernstroms argued that blacks are to blame for many of their educational problems and that there is little racism in America today.[2]

Thernstrom's stand against black students at Harvard was featured in one of the essential neocon books of the nineties, Dinesh D'Souza's *Illiberal Education,* which spent nine weeks on the bestseller list in 1991, promising readers an encyclopedia of offenses perpetrated on campuses in the name of "political correctness." Reviewers of the book highlighted the Thernstrom case as one of D'Souza's most illuminating. Eugene Genovese wrote in the *New Republic* that Thernstrom had been "savaged for political incorrectness in the classroom." *New York* magazine featured Thernstrom as a victim of "demagogic and fanatical" black students. C. Vann Woodward, writing in the *New York Review,* cited the Thernstrom case as an example of "the attack on freedom . . . led by minorities."[3]

The Thernstrom story, as told by D'Souza, is about a distinguished historian who was charged by three black students with "racial insensitivity" in his lectures for an introductory history course, "The Peopling of America." Instead of coming to him with their complaints, Thernstrom told D'Souza, they went to an administrative committee and to the student newspaper, the *Harvard Crimson.* The greatest damage to Thernstrom, he said, was done not by the black students, but by the Harvard administration: Dean of the College Fred Jewett, according to Thernstrom, issued a statement that, "far from coming to his defense, appeared to give full administrative sanction to the charges against Thernstrom." Dean of the Faculty Michael Spence eventually stated that, in D'Souza's words, "no disciplinary action would be taken against Thernstrom," but Spence did "praise the course of action of Thernstrom's accusers as 'judicious and fair.'"[4]

Thernstrom said he was so discouraged by the student attack and the administration's failure to defend his academic freedom that he decided not to teach the course again. Thus the Thernstrom case provided D'Souza, Woodward, Genovese, and others with what they said was an example of a distinguished professor hounded out of teaching his course by an alliance of militant black students and the administrators who supported them: Thernstrom called it "McCarthyism of the Left."[5]

In fact, almost every element of the story Thernstrom told D'Souza was erroneous. The incident in question consisted of three black students complaining about one lecture in a semester-long course. "I talked with one of the students who had complained about Thernstrom," Orlando Patterson, professor of sociology at Harvard, told me. "She was genuinely upset about one of his lectures. This was not an ideological reaction; it was a personal and emotional one. She said she did not want to make it a political issue, and had deliberately rejected attempts by more political students to make it into a cause. She was trembling with rage at the *Crimson* for making this public. She said that when Thernstrom was lecturing on the black family, she understood him to be asking why black men treat their women so badly. I assumed that he had offered a straightforward statement of sociological fact. I told her it's increasingly problematic to have an objective discussion of the black family. We talked for a long time, and in the end, she came around to seeing what I was trying to say. I told her I was sure Steve wasn't a racist, and suggested she go talk to him about how she felt. She did. They had a long talk, shook hands, and that was the end of it. But the *Crimson* made it into a political issue."[6]

Paula Ford was one of the students who complained about Thernstrom; after graduating, she went on to Harvard Law School and then to Washington D.C., where she serves as senior counsel to the Senate Communications Subcommittee. Although Thernstrom told D'Souza that the students never complained directly to him, she told me she and several of her friends talked to Thernstrom after class "a couple of times"—especially after his lecture on the black family. She recalled that "he said black men beat their wives, and then their wives kicked them out. We complained to him after class that this was offensive and inaccurate. He said, 'If you don't believe me, read Toni Morrison.' I felt that was completely trivializing what's out there." She and one other student then went to the campus race relations committee and said, "We have this problem, how do we deal with this?" After the events, she told me, "it was a difficult and emotional process for us. We knew we were dealing with respected tenured professors. A good part of the campus felt, 'They're professors. Why are you accusing them?'"[7]

Regarding Thernstrom's decision not to teach the course again, Ford said she was "surprised" and "not happy" to hear it. "That was not our goal. Our goal was to point out areas in his lectures that we thought were inaccurate and possibly could be changed. To me it's a big overreaction for him to decide not to teach the course again because of that."

Wendi Grantham was described by D'Souza as one of the students who complained about Thernstrom. She graduated in 1989, and went on to study drama in New York City, and later star in the HBO series *The Wire,* the police drama set in Baltimore. "I was not one of the students who filed the complaint," she told me. "I didn't even know they were filing a complaint. A reporter for the *Crimson* led me to believe this complaint was public, which turned out not to be true. All I said was that I could see that their complaint might have some basis."[8]

Eventually she wrote a letter to the *Crimson,* explaining her position. She criticized the *Crimson* coverage and stated categorically, "I do not charge that he is a racist." She pointed out that "no one has silenced or censored him," and she criticized him not for his lectures, but because afterwards he "proclaimed himself victim, and resorted to childish name-calling and irrational comparisons." She concluded, reasonably, that his use of the terms "McCarthyism of the left" and "witch-hunt" were "more than a little extreme."[9]

When I interviewed her, she told me, "People don't understand the term 'racial insensitivity'. It's not a charge of bigotry or racism." She reiterated that she had said in her letter to the *Crimson,* "I do not charge that he is a racist." She added, "We did question some things in his course because his perspective on black life came across to us as simplistic and not reflective of our own experience. You can't always anticipate other people's experience, but you can learn from listening to them. In most academic situations, the professor puts out the knowledge and that's it. But I think some things ought to be questioned."

Thernstrom told D'Souza that black students criticized the course for using slave-owners' journals; D'Souza quoted him saying, "It is essential for young people to hear what justifications the slave owners supplied for their actions."[10] "I agree completely with that," Grantham said. "The problem I had was with the absence of the slave perspective to put alongside the planter perspective. Why not read the slave narratives to get the other side of the story? There's lots of them available, but Prof. Thernstrom didn't assign any. This was a general studies course; for most white students, this was all the black history they would ever get. We felt the knowledge this course would give them was inadequate."

"I finally did go speak to Prof. Thernstrom," she said. "I said I was sorry if he was scapegoated, I did not want to penalize him, but I did want to raise questions about his perspective. It was never my intention to stop Thernstrom from teaching this course. If that's what he chooses to do, it's his decision."

The strongest criticism from Thernstrom (and from D'Souza, Woodward, and Genovese), was aimed not at the black students who complained, but rather at the Harvard administration for its conduct in the Thernstrom case. Because he received so little support from the administration, Thernstrom said, "I felt like a rape victim."[11]

What was this metaphorical rape? "A few days after the Thernstrom incident," D'Souza wrote, "Dean of the College Fred Jewett issued an open letter to the Harvard community. . . . Far from coming to his defense, Jewett appeared to give full administrative sanction to the charges against Thernstrom."[12]

Jewett served as dean of the college at Harvard from 1985 to 1995. "My statement had nothing to do with Thernstrom," he told me. "As I recall it was distributed in registration envelopes at beginning of term, a couple of weeks before anything about Thernstrom became news. It was titled 'Open Letter on Racial Harassment.' There had been some incidents on campus of swastika paintings, and a few incidents involving the police, that had created some concerns.

So we felt we needed a strong general statement on harassment. Obviously, the Thernstrom case was not in that category. When students disagree with the ideas presented by a professor, they are not dealing with harassment; they are dealing with academic freedom. That's not something that the university should interfere with."[13]

The other administrator criticized by Thernstrom was Dean of the Faculty A. Michael Spence—today an emeritus professor and former graduate dean of the business school at Stanford. He won the Nobel Prize for Economics in 2001. Dean Spence was indicted by Thernstrom's defenders because he "praised [Thernstrom's] accusers as 'judicious and fair.'" That charge left out the crucial part of the dean's statement. Dean Spence said that the students who complained "have avoided public comment. . . . That course of action seems to me judicious and fair."[14] It was not the criticism of Thernstrom that was "judicious and fair," but rather the students' decision *not* to go public with their criticism that the dean praised.

Thernstrom charged that, in the same statement, the dean declared "no disciplinary action would be taken" against Thernstrom. In fact, the issue of disciplinary action against Thernstrom was not mentioned in the dean's statement. On the contrary, the dean stated that "in disputes over classroom material . . . instructors exercise full discretion over the content of lectures and the conduct of classroom discussion," and "in the classroom, our students are entitled to question views with which they disagree," and finally "the University cannot prevent all of the conflicts that a commitment to free inquiry may provoke." Thernstrom said he found this statement to be "equivocal at best," interpreting it to mean "he had the right to be a racist, if he wished."[15]

As for the three students who took their complaint to the university's Advisory Committee on Race Relations, what in fact happened was that they were advised that the committee had no jurisdiction over professors' teaching, and that they should take their complaint to Thernstrom—which they did. "They felt the university didn't do anything to back up their concerns," Dean Jewett said.

If D'Souza's account of the Thernstrom case is misleading, it's a model of restraint compared to the other principal account of the same events. *New York* magazine began its article on the case with what appeared to be a description of black students verbally harassing Thernstrom as he walked around the campus: " 'Racist.' 'Racist!' 'The man is a racist!' 'A racist!' Such denunciations, hissed in tones of self-righteousness and contempt, vicious and vengeful, furious, smoking with hatred—such denunciations haunted Stephan Thernstrom for weeks."[16]

When I asked Thernstrom if this passage was accurate, he replied, "I was appalled when I first saw that. Nothing like that ever happened." He described that passage as "artistic license, describing how it felt to be Thernstrom in that period, and that part is absolutely true." He felt that way, he said, because the *Crimson* "ran a story just about every day, with headlines like 'Thernstrom's racial insensitivity still in doubt.' "[17] It's not hard to understand why he would be upset and angry about the *Crimson,* but in fact most of the articles there defended him. It's more significant that he never publicly criticized the completely false description of campus events in *New York* magazine.

According to Thernstrom and his defenders, the final result of black student complaints was that, in the words of *New York* magazine, his course "is no longer offered at Harvard." But that was only because Thernstrom himself decided not to offer it. No black student, or organization, ever demanded, much less suggested, that Thernstrom not teach the course.

Nevertheless, Thernstrom describes himself as a victim of "McCarthyism of the Left."[18] In Thernstrom's case, three students complained that he had been "racially insensitive" in one of his lectures, and he responded by refusing to teach the course again. Under McCarthyism, professors didn't voluntarily decide not to teach a course after being criticized by a few students; they were prevented from teaching all their courses—fired—after being criticized by the government.

Thernstrom, in our 1991 interview, agreed with several of these points. The students who complained about him "wanted to keep it a secret," he said. The administration gave them no satisfaction: "They were told, 'we don't take complaints against the faculty, have you talked to him? If not, do so.' That was the end." The students eventually did come to see him; one meeting "was very formal and cold," while the other was "quite a nice conversation." He agreed that no one had asked, much less demanded, that he not teach the course. He said it was correct that he did not assign slave narratives, because "my focus is more demographic and economic."

As for the administration's public statements, he said that Dean of the Faculty Spence was "very sympathetic; his end-of-the-year report was very strong"—even though D'Souza reported that Thernstrom regarded Spence's statement as "equivocal at best." As for Dean Jewett's statement on racial harassment, "Later I heard that his document had been in the works for a long time and was not issued as some kind of comment on this matter at all." He said he still wasn't certain, and had never asked Jewett—even though D'Souza reported that Jewett "issued the 'open letter' against Thernstrom."

I asked Thernstrom whether he thought black students had criticized him because of his stand on affirmative action. "I am critical of affirmative action," he said, "but I don't think that was clear to them. I didn't lecture on affirmative action. They didn't know what I thought. The complaint was purely internal to the course."

Thernstrom said he remained incensed that Assistant Dean of the College for Minority Affairs Hilda Hernandez-Gravelle "helped these students" prepare their complaint. "I've made clear my dislike for her and her role, and have taken to monitoring her program 'Aware Week,'" he said. "I made an appearance at a couple of the 'Aware' sessions to make it clear that I'm keeping an eye on them."

Hernandez-Gravelle told me, "I think it's really sad that a person would use his energy in such a persecutory and uncollegial manner. This office is about creating dialogue, helping everyone understand different perspectives and ways of recognizing and appreciating the issues. It's appropriate for me to advise and assist students by presenting them with the alternatives they have in addressing their issues. Without commenting specifically on this case, I can say I may help a student write a letter if that is appropriate; I may suggest that it is not necessarily appropriate to accuse a person of being a racist; it might be better to inform him of your reaction to something he said."[19]

I asked Thernstrom what he had wanted the Harvard administration to do, beyond issuing statements affirming his academic freedom. President Derek Bok, he replied, might have "declared that Harvard selects its faculty with enormous care and backs with great confidence the freedom of its professors to discuss subjects in which they are competent"; the administration "might have come out swinging" at the black students who criticized him, Thernstrom said.

Thus the story Thernstrom told in the bestselling account of his case rests on a morass of inaccuracies, exaggerations, and falsehoods. John Womack, who had been chair of the History Department before the complaint against Thernstrom surfaced, commented, "There had been a case years ago at Harvard involving Richard Hernstein, who had his classroom disrupted and was harassed in the Yard [by students who objected to his writing about race and IQ]. But nobody did anything to Steve except say he had been insensitive. You'd think, 'Jesus, he ought to be able to get over that.' Instead Steve just weirded out. He became very combative. He acted as if his entire reputation as a liberal was being wiped out. It's easy to see why the *New Republic* picked it up, but why Gene Genovese or Vann Woodward would get on the bandwagon is more puzzling. To my amazement, this has now become an issue that stands in the annals of free speech."[20]

"There is no Thernstrom case," concluded Martin Kilson, professor of government at Harvard. "There were 680 black students at Harvard at the time. A couple of them complained about his interpretations of the black experience. That got translated into an attack on freedom of speech by black students. Nothing like that ever happened at Harvard. It's a marvelous example of the skill of the neocons at taking small events and translating them into weapons against the pluralistic thrust on American campuses."[21]

The Thernstrom story was thus written as the story of a historian in trouble because of charges of racism—charges that were unfair. But nobody charged Thernstrom with racism. A few black students felt he had been "insensitive" in one of his lectures, and they went to talk to him about it—precisely what students, and professors, ought to do. The student newspaper published several articles about the events, a majority of which defended Thernstrom.[22] The problem here is not with what Thernstrom said in his lecture about the black family, or with his meeting students who disagreed with his interpretation. The problem came afterwards, when he turned these minor events into a cause célèbre for the right, describing himself as a victim of left-wing political correctness.

So the Harvard professor who said he "felt like a rape victim" after he was criticized by three black female students, who said the Harvard administration should have "come out swinging" at the three black women who had challenged a lecture of his—that professor was appointed by President George W. Bush to the National Council on the Humanities. The *Crimson,* reporting on his nomination, went to Thernstrom for a quote. He said that, if he had acquired any "wisdom" in teaching, he "hoped to apply it . . . as a member of the Council."[23] Presumably that included the wisdom he gained in teaching "The Peopling of America" to those three black students.

II

Targeted by the Right

4

Arming America *and* "*Academic Fraud*"

*M*ichael Bellesiles, accused of having committed academic fraud in his book *Arming America,* received the academic equivalent of lethal injection—after Emory University found him guilty of "falsification," he resigned from his tenured position as a full professor. Since then he has taught in England and returned to Atlanta, where he's been working on a book for Oxford University Press on the history of violence in America. Before that, the Bellesiles case had been a major media event. A search of the Lexis-Nexis database produced 234 articles on Bellesiles published in the two years before July 2003, including seven in the *New York Times.*[1]

The Bellesiles case raises two questions: was he guilty of fraud or merely error? And what is the appropriate punishment for the offenses of which he was guilty? The problem is that some historians whose offenses were more serious, and against whom the evidence was more damning, received little or no punishment. It's hard to escape the conclusion that Bellesiles's problem was not just sloppy research and inadequate notekeeping; Bellesiles's problem was that his book provoked a powerful, vocal, and well-organized constituency that succeeded at putting pressure on his university, his publisher, and the history profession. That constituency was the gun lobby.

The problems found by many scholars in Bellesiles's work were serious ones. The most basic problem was inadequate documentation, especially of his data on gun ownership in early America coming from probate records. The basic principle of documentation for all scholarship is that footnotes should enable readers to locate the sources cited in the text, and footnotes should enable readers to retrace the steps of the author to use data as evidence for an argument. When Bellesiles wrote that only 15 percent of adult white men in America owned guns before 1790, the reader should have been able to find out how he arrived at that figure.

For that argument, Bellesiles relied on probate records—inventories and wills—and reported finding that surprisingly few people listed guns in their estates or willed guns to heirs. In a footnote to the table reporting his findings, he listed forty county courthouses across the country where he had found probate records in the archives. But his note was incomplete: he failed to indicate how he carried out his research, and what his methods were. As the editor of the *Journal of American History* later wrote, "He failed to include the sample size in each of the table's cells, to indicate which counties were used to construct each regional category, and to note the exact locations of the county records used."[2] Many scholarly works have incomplete or sketchy notes to tables. Bellesiles's book as a whole is massively footnoted and documented, with 125 pages of notes at the end. However, the argument that few people owned guns in early America was so striking and so significant that he owed it to his readers to explain his research methodology fully and completely. (In his response to critics in the *William and Mary Quarterly,* he concedes these points, and in the second edition of the book, he includes appropriate documentation for a revised Table 1.)

Most of the rest of the published criticism of Bellesiles that came from historians concerned issues of interpretation. The most important issues were raised in a forum in the distinguished *William and Mary Quarterly,* where four historians commented on different parts of Bellesiles's book and he responded. Gloria L. Main concluded her essay, "If historians want to pin our 'gun culture' on capitalism, then capitalism itself came early to our shores"—"in the first ships" that landed in seventeenth-century Plymouth and Virginia.[3] That's a challenge to Bellesiles's argument that gun culture developed along with the rise of manufacturing and mass marketing in the mid-nineteenth century. It's a difference of interpretation, the kind of debate that makes history interesting; it's not a cause for disciplinary proceedings or ending careers.

Ira Gruber argued in his essay that Bellesiles "overemphasized the weaknesses of the militia" and "created too pacific a description of life in Britain's American colonies."[4] Again, this is a debate over emphasis and interpretation. Randolph Roth pointed out that no other researchers had come up with figures on guns and homicide similar to Bellesiles's, and concluded Bellesiles has made errors in his calculations.[5] How serious were these errors, and what is the appropriate penalty?

To understand the problem of the Bellesiles case, it's necessary to examine the official proceedings at Emory in the larger context of the organized campaign against him and the publicity it received, and then consider similar cases with different conclusions. *Arming America,* published by Knopf in September 2000, argued that our picture of guns in early America is all wrong: the picture where America was settled by men with guns in their hands, hunting game and fighting Indians, where in 1776 militiamen grabbed their guns to go fight for independence, where the Founding Fathers protected individuals' right to own guns. Bellesiles argued instead that gun culture is a fairly recent development in American history. For two centuries before the Civil War, relatively few Americans owned guns; the guns they had were unreliable and didn't shoot straight; few people hunted with guns, instead relying on trapping and animal husbandry; even in battle, even in the Revolutionary War, swords, axes, and fire were more deadly than guns. Not until the Civil War put guns in the hands of millions of men did gun culture flourish. Because of Bellesiles's striking thesis and research, his book won the prestigious Bancroft Prize in 2000, awarded by Columbia University for the best research in American history.

The political implications of Bellesiles's book were significant for the NRA: the Second Amendment, this suggested, was not adopted to protect the widespread ownership or popularity of guns—it was instead intended to address the inadequacy of the weapons in the hands of local militias, on which the early nation relied in the absence of a standing army. While the book is focused exclusively on the eighteenth and nineteenth centuries with virtually no references to implications for the present, Bellesiles's introduction included a fierce attack on Charleton Heston and the NRA.

Even before *Arming America* was published, the NRA targeted Bellesiles and his book. Initially the campaign was restricted to gun websites and publications on the right like the *National Review* and the *Weekly Standard,* but eventually some historians began examining Bellesiles's research. His initial responses to inquiries succeeded only in provoking further questions; Emory University appointed a three-person panel of distinguished historians to investigate the charges against him. It was their report that led to his resignation.

Several leading historians turned down an invitation to serve on Emory's external review committee, even though they were offered $10,000.[6] The people who accepted the invitation were Stanley Katz, former head of the American Council of Learned Societies and a Princeton faculty member; Hannah H. Gray, former president of the University of Chicago; and Harvard professor Laurel Thatcher Ulrich, MacArthur fellow and winner of the Pulitzer Prize for her book *A Midwife's Tale.*[7]

The committee concluded that Bellesiles's research into probate records was "unprofessional and misleading" as well as "superficial and thesis-driven," and that his earlier explanations of errors "raise doubts about his veracity." But they found "evidence of falsification" only on one page: Table 1, "Percentage of probate inventories listing firearms." From a table that covered almost a century—1765 to 1859—Bellesiles omitted two years: 1774 and 1775. These years would have shown more guns.[8]

But the committee made a serious mistake at the outset of their work: they agreed to limit their report to answering five narrow questions posed by the Emory University administration, and to avoid the larger issues of the significance of their findings. They also avoided any comment on what sanctions, if any, would be appropriate. The result was a report marred by a kind of tunnel vision.

Gray, Katz, and Ulrich also refused to answer qustions about the significance of their findings when asked directly. Ulrich's e-mail response to me was characteristic: "I'm sure you can understand why it wouldn't be appropriate for me to comment."[9]

In fact, the probate records criticized by the committee are referred to only in a handful of paragraphs in a 400-page book, and Table 1 is cited in the text only a couple of times. If Bellesiles had omitted all of the probate data that the committee and others have criticized, the book's argument would remain a strong one, supported by a wide variety of other evidence that the committee did not challenge.

What is the appropriate penalty for omitting 1774 and 1775 from Table 1? Gray, Katz, and Ulrich did not say in their report, and refused to answer when I asked them. Before the report was completed, Emory officials had told me the possibilities ranged from a letter of reprimand to demotion to termination.[10] Was any action by Bellesiles's employer justified—or is the harsh criticism Bellesiles has received from within the profession penalty enough? Again, when I asked them, the committee members refused to answer.

Bellesiles in his official reply to the committee explained that he omitted 1774 and 1775 not to deceive readers, but because he thought those years were not relevant to his thesis: "the colonial governments were passing out firearms to the members of their militia . . . in preparation for the expected confrontation with Great Britain"; therefore these two years give "an inaccurate portrait of peacetime gun ownership" by individuals.[11] If Bellesiles had stated that in a note to Table 1, would the committee have found no "evidence of falsification"? They declined to answer.

How bad is Bellesiles's Table 1? I asked a colleague who teaches quantitative history to graduate students and who is a strong advocate of teaching "numeracy" as part of the curriculum. "It's not bad," he said. "I've seen a lot worse in books published by leading university presses. He could have disaggregated his data a bit, which would have been a good idea."

Indeed, Bellesiles conceded serious problems in his probate data, and spent the next year working on correcting his errors for a second edition of the book, which was published in September 2003. The book includes a corrected version of Table 1, with much more detail: it disaggregates the data by county and also shows the total number of probate records and the number with guns for each county in each of six multi-year periods. The revised table includes fewer counties, and shows more guns—for the period 1765–90, for example, the national total is 22 percent of probate inventories listing guns, compared to 15 percent in the original version. The new Table 1 also refers readers to the author's website "for the name of every probate file examined as well as the exact description and valuation of every firearm."[12] Do Gray, Katz, and Ulrich consider that an appropriate resolution of the problems they found in the original Table 1? They refused to say.

The context of the debate over *Arming America* is crucial to understanding the problems with the committee's report. Gun rights groups had been working to discredit the book and destroy Bellesiles's career since before the book was published—they saw it as "anti-gun," partly because the introduction criticized Charleton Heston and the NRA.

By accepting the terms of debate set by others, Gray, Katz, and Ulrich abdicated their intellectual responsibility to work independently and to consider the significance of their findings. As a result, their report had ominous implications for other historians dealing with controversial issues. Of course, every historian has an obligation to provide full and accurate citations of evidence in a form that makes it possible for others to replicate their work. But I know of one historian coming up for tenure who, after reading the Emory report on Bellesiles, decided to remove all the tables from his book manuscript, to treat the evidence anecdotally instead, in order to avoid facing the same kind of critique.

Since the issue here was Bellesiles's integrity as a historian, the Emory inquiry should have been as sweeping as the stakes, instead of being tied to a few pages in a big book. And if Bellesiles was right in his reply, then Gray, Katz, and Ulrich are guilty of some of the same sins they accuse him of committing: suppressing inconvenient evidence, spinning the data their way, refusing to follow leads that didn't serve their thesis. The point is not to condemn them for their inability to achieve the scrupulousness they demanded of

Bellesiles. The point is that historians have to deal with the messy confusion of things, and they offer interpretations of it. Historian Michael Zuckerman of the University of Pennsylvania told me, "Historical knowledge advances by the testing of interpretations, not by stifling interpreters"—and not by indicting the interpreter's character for flaws in his Table 1.[13]

The campaign against Bellesiles was fought on many fronts. When he came to the University of California, Irvine, to give a talk on the controversy surrounding his book—this was in 2001, before he was charged with inventing evidence, and before he was awarded the Bancroft Prize—people coming to the talk were greeted at the door of the lecture hall by a couple of unusually large men passing out a brochure titled "The Lies of Michael Bellesiles." One had a shaved head, another wore a leather coat on a warm day; they did not look like history grad students or faculty members. People coming to the talk were startled, and some were a little frightened, but Bellesiles said calmly, "Ah, so they did come."[14]*

*After this section was published in *The Nation,* the editors received an e-mail that read, "I was one of the several large men . . . that Jon Weiner [sic] referred to in his article. . . . I admit to being a tall, middle-aged man who is obese, due to recently-diagnosed insulin resistance that has now led to Type II diabetes. Another of my middle-aged friends who attended Dr. Bellesiles's talk, also overweight and identified by Jon Weiner as having a shaved head (implying my friend is a Nazi skinhead), lost most of the hair on his head due to alopecia. . . . I don't remember what my 77-year-old Jewish mother, also in attendance with us, was wearing." J. Neil Schulman, e-mail to the editor of *The Nation* [unpublished], October 19, 2002, in author's possession.

In his talk, Bellesiles described how John James Audubon was accused in 1831 by his enemies of fraud in a painting of a rattlesnake climbing a tree to a bird's nest—because, they said, rattlesnakes can't climb trees; and how, even though Audubon proved rattlesnakes could climb trees, nothing he said or wrote persuaded his critics because their goal was to discredit and destroy his work. Bellesiles said his own experience was similar—even when he answered one of his critics' charges fully and completely, they still repeated the same charge over and over.

When the question period came, he started with the first of the large men. "You say the probate records show very few guns, and argue that this proves people in early America didn't have guns. But when my father died, there was nothing in his will about his guns—even though he owned four of them. But he had told me he wanted me to have them, and now I do. Are probate records really a good source of evidence on gun ownership?"

Bellesiles answered, "I'm sure you're right about your father's will, but wills in the eighteenth century were different. People didn't own very many things compared to today, and their wills contained a detailed list of everything they had, down to the knives and forks. There are other problems with probate records; they are biased in many ways. But I'm confident that if an eighteenth century man owned a gun, it would be in his will. Remember that we're talking here about wills in the 1700s."

He called on the second large man. "I want to ask about your use of probate records," he said. "You say probate records showed few guns, but my father owned several guns that did not appear in his will when he died. My brother and I divided them up."

Bellesiles paused and looked around the room, where students glanced at each other with stunned disbelief: so this is what it's like when you're the target of a campaign to destroy your work.

The campaign against *Arming America* started with the NRA and gun websites, and then went to the *Wall Street Journal,* the *New Criterion,* the *Weekly Standard,* and the *National Review,* which challenged the book's evidence and conclusions.[15]

Historians who wrote positive reviews of the book were bombarded with belligerent e-mail urging them to reverse their opinions and publicly retract their reviews; a campaign was launched to pressure the Columbia University trustees to withdraw the Bancroft Prize he had been awarded; the National Endowment for the Humanities in May 2002 had its name removed from a $30,000 fellowship Bellesiles was completing in Chicago; Bellesiles himself was the target of hate mail and death threats; and finally, the campaign demanded that Emory University fire him.[16]

This campaign aimed at a book which had received high praise from some of the top historians in America: Garry Wills wrote in the *New York Times Book Review,* "Bellesiles has dispersed the darkness that covered the gun's early history in America."[17] Edmund Morgan, the award-winning Yale historian, wrote in the *New York Review,* "No one else has put [the facts] together in so compelling a refutation of the mythology of the gun or in so revealing a reconstruction of the role the gun has actually played in American history."[18] And there was the Bancroft Prize, awarded annually by Columbia University to the best books in American history.

While the campaign against the book began as a politically motivated effort by the gun lobby and its supporters, it expanded to include several scholars and historians, who devoted weeks and months to checking Bellesiles's footnotes in the archives—a practice which is extremely unusual in historical scholarship. They found that there were indeed some problems, especially with Bellesiles's notes to probate records.

Bellesiles readily agreed, and offered an explanation: a flood in April 2000 at the history office building at Emory destroyed his notes on the probate records (and also seriously damaged most of the rest of the offices). The university said the damage totaled a million dollars. Bellesiles's text was safe, but the probate notes were on yellow legal pads on a chair—admittedly an archaic mode of record storage—rather than on computer, and the wet ceiling tiles fell down and, he said, turned the yellow pads to "unreadable pulp." After the flood, he went to work trying to recreate the notes, and when his book was published that September, he posted notices on several history websites that his original notes on the probate records had been destroyed. The schedule here is crucial: Bellesiles did not come up with a story about a flood destroying his records in response to critics; he published his report about the flood first, several months before critics focused on problems in the documentation for his Table 1.[19]

However, it bears repeating that the probate records played an extremely small part in the book's argument. The index referred to only twelve paragraphs where probate records were even mentioned, scattered throughout the book. One of these was a discussion of biases in probate records. That's twelve paragraphs in a book that's 600 pages long. The book relied on many different kinds of sources, all of them familiar to historians—newspapers, private letters and official correspondence, memoirs and diaries, travel accounts, army records, and police and criminal court files.

Nevertheless, the checking of Bellesiles's probate data became a mammoth undertaking for his critics, and eventually for the Emory committee. Leading the pack was James Lindgren, a law professor at Northwestern University who (with Justin Lee Heather) published a critique of the probate data in the *William and Mary Law Review*. Their article on Bellesiles's one-page table on probate records ran sixty-six pages, with 189 footnotes. They reported some interesting numbers: more people listed guns in early wills than swords or bibles. They reported finding more guns, and more in good condition, than Bellesiles did. They concluded that Bellesiles "substantially misrecorded the 17th and 18th century data" on the number of gun owners.[20]

But the gun-counters avoided the most significant issue Bellesiles raised, as Jack Rakove, a distinguished historian at Stanford, argued. "Even if a substantial portion or even a majority of households possessed guns, genuine questions about their use would remain," he wrote in the *William and Mary Quarterly* issue devoted to the controversy. The key question here was "whether ordinary citizens had the skill to use firearms effectively."[21] Bellesiles had good evidence that gun-owners had trouble maintaining their weapons and little experience in using guns, which were inaccurate and unreliable in most cases. One of my favorite examples: of the famous Minutemen at Lexington Green in 1775, only seven actually fired their muskets, and only one Redcoat was actually hit.[22]

*   *   *

The charges of "fraud" raised by Lindgren and dozens of others (including Alexander Cockburn in *The Nation*) focused on one footnote, to that same Table 1 in the appendix to *Arming America,* which listed forty counties around the United States as sources of probate records—including San Francisco.[23] That seemed unlikely to many historians, who know the San Francisco archives were destroyed in the 1906 earthquake and fire. After the flood destroyed his notes, Bellesiles had recreated from memory the list of the forty counties where he researched probate records. At this point, he reported, he went back to San Francisco and found the critics were right in arguing there were no probate records in the archives of San Francisco County.

But the critics were wrong in charging that he had invented the documents. He found the documents in question across the bay, in the Contra Costa County archives. He xeroxed and distributed copies of the documents in question, and posted examples on his website.[24] They are indeed headed "City and County of San Francisco." The Contra Costa archivists confirmed that the documents were real—and that they came from the Contra Costa County archives, not San Francisco.[25] Bellesiles did not invent documents; he gave the wrong location for the documents in question. That's error, not fraud.

You might think that would end the discussion. But the attacks over the "San Francisco" probate records took on a life of their own. The director of the Contra Costa County Historical Society told inquiring reporters that Bellesiles had never been to that archive, because his name did not appear on the sign-in sheet. New charges of fraud ricocheted around the gun websites, the history e-mail lists, and the media, including the Chicago *Tribune*.[26] Bellesiles explained simply that he had not signed in. (Tightly run archives don't give anyone access without signing in, but many smaller local historical societies rely on volunteers who are not as strict.) Amid new demands that Columbia University take back his Bancroft Prize and that Emory fire him, few noticed the conclusion Bellesiles drew from the "San Francisco" documents: "probate records from the late 1850s reinforce the portrait of increased gun use in America."[27] Those fifteen words were the only reference to "San Francisco" probate records in the 600-page book—and none of the critics disagreed with those fifteen words.[28]

While the probate materials and especially the "San Francisco" documents aroused the most attention, critics attacked other parts of Bellesiles's book as well, especially his argument that few murders were committed with guns in early America. The energetic Lindgren published a second attack on Bellesiles in the *Yale Law Review*—this one was fifty-four pages with 247 footnotes. He joined Randolph Roth (who wrote on the same topic in the *William and Mary Quarterly*)[29] in declaring that Bellesiles had "a 100% error rate in finding homicide cases in the Plymouth [Colony] records."[30] But Mary Beth Norton, a prize-winning historian of early America who has worked in those records, went back and checked them for this debate; she told me that Bellesiles's interpretation of the documents was "just as plausible" as his critics', "if not more so."[31]

Lindgren did not limit his contributions to law review publications. As the *Chronicle of Higher Education* pointed out, he was "virtually ubiquitous" in the media write-ups of the controversy. He distributed his attack brief to journalists, and, the *Chronicle* reported at the time, "talks to them—a lot."[32] He provided writers, including this one, with lists of anti-Bellesiles academics who could be called for quotes, along with their contact information, and suggestions about how the story should be written.[33]

Lindgren has also contacted historians who had written positive reviews of *Arming America* and, according to the *Chronicle*, "urged them to reconsider their positions—in print."[34] This is pretty much unheard of in academia. Matthew Warshauer reviewed the book in the journal *Connecticut History*. He told me that Lindgren asked him to publish a retraction. "He added something like he would hate to have this affect my career. I viewed that as a veiled threat." Warshauer was an untenured assistant professor at Central Connecticut State University. "I have twelve e-mails Lindgren sent me," he said, "including little ones, like 'where are you at with this?' He definitely kept up the pressure."[35]

Who is James Lindgren? He accused Bellesiles of bias, but apparently has some ideological bias of his own. Before he wrote his two articles on guns, he published an article using data gathered by the right-wing Federalist Society that purported to prove the American Bar Association had been biased against George W. Bush's judicial nominees. But his methodology was exposed as deeply flawed in an article in the *Journal of Law & Politics* co-authored by a law professor who is co-editor of the book *Modern Scientific Evidence*.[36] These are his major law review articles in the last four years. His only other significant publication in recent years was a survey of academics' views, "Rating the Presidents."[37]

One of the most disturbing elements in the story concerns the *William and Mary Quarterly*. Its editors asked prominent historians, including Randolph Roth, to criticize Bellesiles, and then invited Bellesiles to respond. In his response, he made the point that everybody makes mistakes, and cited an error in Randolph Roth's article—Roth referred to what he said was information from the Plymouth Colony records of a murder, but in fact, Bellesiles said, that page was a record of births. But before publication, the editors corrected the error in Roth's article and deleted Bellesiles's argument from his response.[38]

The campaign by gun activists, in contrast, was openly vitriolic. The website Shooters.com reported on the "San Francisco" documents story and concluded "Everything Bellesiles wrote is false, bogus, a big lie."[39] KeepAndBearArms.com had a page headlined "Michael A. Bellesiles: Mega Anti-Gun-Nut—Part XVI."[40] That website posted a link to Matthew Warshauer's graduate history seminar at Central Connecticut where Bellesiles's book was assigned, and encouraged gun supporters to e-mail Warshauer. The editor of the Keep and Bear Arms website, Angel Shamaya, himself e-mailed Warshauer, "If you're planning on exposing Bellesiles as the lying sack of anti-gun excrement he is, good for you. . . . But if, on the other hand, you're planning to pretend that . . . he is anything less than a deceitful snake—you're unfit to teach."[41]

Probably we shouldn't be surprised by the vehemence of the book's critics—not after the decade of the culture wars.[42] In many cases, the attacks on Bellesiles came from the usual suspects who have made careers out of bashing the left: Ronald Radosh wrote about Bellesiles on David Horowitz's website, Harvey Klehr wrote in the *New Criterion.* The *National Review* devoted several articles to Bellesiles and ran additional updates on their website. The NRA has been after Bellesiles since before publication of the book: Charleton Heston, president of the NRA, denounced Bellesiles in 1999, declaring in *Guns and Ammo* magazine that the historian had "too much time on his hands," and later in a letter to the *New York Times,* calling Bellesiles's book "ludicrous."[43]

But there have been some surprises. One of the more original critics challenged Bellesiles's account of the damage done by the flood in his Emory office building. Professor Jerome Sternstein of Brooklyn College put a dozen legal pads in his own shower for thirty minutes and reported to the world that they survived "intact and virtually unscathed."[44] Then there is Clayton Cramer, a gun activist and amateur historian who savaged Bellesiles on the *National Review* website and who wrote about him regularly for *Shotgun News;* Cramer's own website invited readers who supported his campaign against Bellesiles to send him money.[45]

The *New Criterion* and the *National Review* portrayed Bellesiles as a typical New Left radical historian—but he's not. He told me he had been a registered Republican, and John McCain supporter in 2000, but had subsequently switched to Democrat. He described himself as a "Burkean conservative" who believed in "tradition and authority," and also as a longtime gun owner who only recently gave up skeet shooting. He told the *Chronicle* he was "rethinking what it means to be a Christian and to own guns."[46]

He won support from leading scholarly organizations, including the American Historical Association and the Organization of American Historians, which passed resolutions deploring the harassment and abuse directed at him.[47] He responded to critics in a variety of academic venues, including the *William and Mary Quarterly* and the newsletter of the Organization of American History.[48]

The mainstream media coverage of the case accelerated after Emory appointed its external review committee. When the university released a statement in August 2002 that "Professor Michael Bellesiles will be on paid leave from his teaching duties at Emory University during the fall semester," no fewer than ten daily newspapers reported the story, including the *Boston Globe*.[49]

Bellesiles's response to the criticism was to publish a second edition of *Arming America*.[50] He spent a lot of time revisiting archives where he had done his original probate research to correct his flawed data. And he wrote a new introduction that omitted the attacks on Charleton Heston and the NRA. The new introduction is strictly historical; it opens with Ben Franklin worrying in 1776 that the colonies lacked guns, and proposing instead that they fight the British with "bows and arrows," which "are more easily provided everywhere than muskets and ammunition." The new introduction also replies to the NRA critics, declaring that his purpose was not to "endorse current efforts at gun control." The new introduction also describes the flood at Emory that destroyed his notes on probate records, and acknowledges as well problems in relying on probate records. He concludes by restating the thesis of the book, that gun culture in America is "an invented tradition," a product of the Civil War era rather than the colonial period.[51] This is the book's real contribution, and it remains a genuinely significant one.

Mary Beth Norton, a prize-winning historian of early America who teaches at Cornell, summed up the case: Bellesiles's use of probate records was "slapdash and sloppy," she told me, but the rest of the criticisms of *Arming America* "strike me as the usual sorts of disagreements historians always have about how to interpret documentary evidence, although those criticisms have been expressed more vehemently than is usual in the scholarly literature."[52]

Michael Zuckerman is professor of history at the University of Pennsylvania. "The critics' stuff on the probate inventories is bad news for Michael," he told me, "but the book in no way depends on that. He's got myriad arguments. If people are so crazy about guns, why are there so few gun sellers? So few gun manufacturers? Why do they need a government subsidy? The critics are casting about for a way to discredit him, and they have fixated on the probate inventories, which is crackpot. They have refused to confront the cumulative force and extent of the argument. In fact the argument is splendid."[53]

Michael Kammen, past president of the Organization of American Historians, has not withdrawn his statement that *Arming America* is "a classic work of significant scholarship with inescapable policy implications." Garry Wills and Edmund Morgan refused demands that they withdraw or alter their published praise for the book. The website for the new edition carries Wills's quote, "Bellesiles has dispersed the darkness that covered the gun's early history in America."[54]

And the debate over the meaning of the Second Amendment is not going to be resolved by Bellesiles or his critics counting guns in early America.

In the end, despite dozens of researchers devoting weeks and months to checking every line in the 125 pages of notes at the end of *Arming America,* the critics came up with no evidence of intentional deception, no evidence of invented documents. The Emory review committee finding that he was guilty of "falsification" referred only to two years omitted from one table, not to the text where the table was discussed.

The procedures Emory followed in the Bellesiles case contrasted sharply with the same university's response to evidence of misconduct by his colleague in the history department Elizabeth Fox-Genovese. In one case, they convened an external review committee of distinguished historians to evaluate the charges against him; in the other, they did nothing.

One of the difficulties in coming to a judgment in the Bellesiles case is what historian Kenneth Pomeranz calls "the baseline problem"—we have no idea what the typical or average rate of error is in historical research, because the only people whose footnotes get checked are those who arouse criticism or opposition—often because of their thesis or political stance rather than the appearance of sloppy note taking.

The campaign against Bellesiles sought not to refute his book's thesis or claims made about its contemporary significance, but instead to discredit it by focusing attention on errors in a tiny portion of the documentation. It's an old tactic, and an illogical one: the book could be wrong about the origins of our present gun culture even if its footnotes were flawless. But the tactic succeeded.

Now Bellesiles is out of the university, working on a new project. If he had published research showing that there were fewer books in early America than previously believed, rather than fewer guns, he might be wrong, but he'd still be teaching history at Emory.

5

David Abraham and the Nazis

What does it take to end the career of an untenured historian? The exemplary case was David Abraham's. In 1985, two senior historians, one at Yale and the other at Berkeley, devoted their time and committed their professional reputations to destroying his career—and succeeded. His book, *The Collapse of the Weimar Republic,* published by Princeton University Press, widely praised in more than thirty reviews, was found to contain numerous errors. Before the Abraham case, debates among scholars occasionally had been vicious, but this was more than a debate: it was a vendetta, and it was unprecedented.[1]

Abraham's critics, led by Professor Henry A. Turner Jr. of Yale and Gerald A. Feldman of Berkeley, sought not just to expose Abraham's errors, but also make sure that he would never get another academic job and to persuade his publisher to withdraw his book. They also argued that the University of Chicago should rescind his Ph.D. Lawrence Stone, then Dodge Professor of History at Princeton, told me at the time, "I've never seen a witch hunt like this in forty years in two countries." Natalie Zemon Davis, at the time Henry Charles Lea Professor of History at Princeton, had seen something like it before: "In some ways," she told me, "it's reminiscent of McCarthyite hysteria."[2]

These events revealed much about the position of Marxism in the history profession in the mid-eighties, about the debate between old-fashioned positivists and interpretive historians over where historical truth lies, and about ethics in academia. In the course of researching and writing his book, Abraham misdated and misattributed one document, mistranslated another document in a way that distorted its meaning, and treated a paraphrase of a third document as a quotation. He was also accused of making dozens of lesser mistakes. Abraham acknowledged his errors in print and apologized for them. His critics, however, were not satisfied. Historian Carl Schorske told me at the time, "They're not saying, 'Here's a serious error.' They're saying 'Here's a lie, and I'll tell you why this guy lies.' "[3] In accusing Abraham of fraud, his critics implied that he had to fabricate documents because his Marxist interpretation could not be sustained by the truth.

Stone, whose major work was in the hotly contested field of seventeenth-century English social history, disputed Feldman's claim that good historians do not make mistakes, especially in their archival research. "When you work in the archives," he told me, "you're far from home, you're bored, you're in a hurry, you're scribbling like crazy. You're bound to make mistakes. I don't believe any scholar in the Western world has impeccable footnotes. Archival research is a special case of the general messiness of life."[4]

Indeed, there was ample evidence that David Abraham was not the single bad apple in a barrel of virtuous footnoters. The publishers of the great British historian Sir Lewis Namier planned a second edition of his masterly *Structure of Politics at the Accession of George III.* When editors checked the footnotes, Lawrence Stone said, "I was told they found endless, constant, minor errors." Emmanuel Le Roy Ladurie, France's most celebrated historian, was criticized by the Vatican librarian in the mid-1980s for mistranslations and other errors in his masterwork *Montaillou.*[5]

Perhaps Abraham's mistakes were more serious than those made by other researchers? "I can't think of another case in which an author's footnotes have been systematically checked in the archives," Stone said. "David's errors seem at the moment to be worse than others', but we can't be sure because nobody else's have been subjected to this kind of systematic scrutiny."[6] Feldman and Turner disagreed; each reported that his own work had been checked—and upheld.

The campaign against Abraham was begun by Turner, a bitter opponent of Marxist history who had been working for years on a defense of German businessmen in the period immediately preceding the rise of Hitler. Turner became furious after hearing Abraham's work praised at a March 1983 colloquium on Weimar history at Harvard University. He wrote a letter attacking the book and sent it, along with photocopies of original documents that he said Abraham had misquoted, to colleagues in the United States and Germany.[7] One of the recipients, Arno Mayer, then Dayton-Stockton Professor of History at Princeton, wrote Turner protesting his private campaign against Abraham. "You vent your anger at David Abraham for daring to publish a book on a topic on which you yourself have been working for years," Mayer wrote. "Have you no shame? Have you no sense of decency?"[8] Feldman, the author of *Iron and Steel in the German Inflation, 1916–1923,* who had read Abraham's manuscript and recommended it for publication, sided with Turner.

Turner went public with his campaign against Abraham in the October 1983 issue of the *American Historical Review.* In a letter alleging that Abraham had forged a document showing business support for Hitler in the last days of Weimar, Turner reminded his colleagues that forgery was "among the gravest of scholarly offenses."[9] It was hard to remember such a serious charge being made against another historian.

Abraham then traveled to West Germany and found the document he had been accused of forging. It had no signature and an imprecise date. He conceded in his *American Historical Review* response that his dating and attribution had been erroneous. Even those who agreed with Abraham's interpretation of Weimar felt that some of his research was sloppy and that his mistakes were not trivial. However, there was a consensus that Abraham had successfully defended himself against the charge of forgery. Turner never apologized or offered a retraction for his allegations, and to many in the profession, he now looked like a man with an ax to grind: his own book had been pre-empted by a younger scholar whose Marxism he despised. At this point Turner ceded the front lines of the battle against Abraham to Feldman.

In 1982, Abraham had been recommended for tenure by the Princeton history department, but the dean's committee turned down the recommendation—not an unusual event in a Princeton tenure case. Thus at the end of 1983, Abraham was on the job market, with a highly praised book, a dossier of references from prestigious historians, and the dispute over his scholarly integrity resolved in his favor. It was then that Feldman began his own campaign of letters and telephone calls to make sure that no university hired Abraham. Feldman's "Dear Colleague" letters were sent to dozens, perhaps hundreds, of historians in the U.S. and Europe. In its scope, methods, and animus, the campaign was unprecedented in the history profession.

The University of Texas at Austin was the first of Feldman's targets. Its history department invited Abraham for an interview, but offered the job to someone else—after hearing from Feldman. Then, after Catholic University's history department voted to recommend hiring Abraham, the department chair began receiving calls from Feldman—four or five in a two-week period, according to Timothy Tackett, a member of the search committee. "We were shocked," Tackett told me at the time. "All his calls were unsolicited. He threatened to go over our heads to the administration."[10]

Among the unsolicited materials Feldman sent was a thirty-page attack on Abraham's scholarship, written by Feldman's former student Ulrich Nocken, a professor at the University of Dusseldorf. Back in 1976, Nocken had applied for the Princeton job that had been given to Abraham. The Nocken essay was "a diatribe," Tackett told me. "Feldman told us it was forthcoming in the *Vieterljahrschrift fur Sozial- und Wirtschaftsgeschichte,* a reputable journal. It was impossible to ignore, but hard to verify in the short time we had. We were fuming, miserable and outraged."[11] Thirteen of the department's fifteen members signed a document urging the administration to go ahead and appoint Abraham, but the dean decided against their recommendation.

The University of California, Santa Cruz, was next. Abraham was a leading candidate for a position there when Feldman intervened. The pattern was the same—four or five telephone calls to the department over the course of a month; the typescript of Nocken's attack; the unsolicited letters; and the threats from Feldman that if the department didn't follow his advice, he would oppose Abraham's appointment at higher levels, including the university's systemwide Board of Regents. "I made it clear," Feldman said, "that I was not going to have Abraham appointed in this university system."[12]

Santa Cruz hired someone else. But thirteen members of the department signed a letter addressed to the American Historical Association, protesting Feldman's interference.

Feldman also wrote Princeton University Press, Abraham's publisher, declaring that Abraham's book was "fraudulent and should be withdrawn from sale," and insisting that it not be advertised "on dust jackets, in journals, and in catalogues." If the press did not comply, Feldman wrote, "you should know that the request will be repeated by me in very choice company and . . . a further decision to continue marketing the book will be made a matter of public record in what I write."[13]

Perhaps the most extreme development in the case concerned Abraham's Ph.D. Feldman thought the University of Chicago should rescind the degree, although when I spoke with him in 1985, he added, "I have not made any such formal proposal up to the present time." Nevertheless, both the history department and the president's office at the university received at least some informal suggestions to that effect. Some time later the president of the university, Hanna H. Gray, filed a protest with the American Historical Association, describing Feldman's actions as a violation of professional norms.[14] Even if Feldman did not make a formal proposal that Chicago strip Abraham of his Ph.D., Feldman told me at the time that he would be happy to join in such an action—especially, he said, if he continued to be "harassed" by Abraham's supporters (presumably like University of Chicago President Hanna Gray) charging him with unethical conduct.

Feldman's duty, as he saw it, had been to alert the profession to what he viewed as Abraham's misconduct. Stanley Katz, at the time Princeton Class of 1921 Bicentennial Professor of the History of American Law and Liberty, who joined in signing Gray's letter of protest to the AHA, disagreed. "Turner's letter to the *American Historical Review* gave the profession sufficient notice of the charges against Abraham," he told me at the time. "It appeared well before any departments were considering hiring David. The burden is on those departments. If they consider it a problem, they may consult Turner or Feldman or others. Indeed, they all were aware of the controversy and worried about it. It has yet to be shown that there's a single example of fabrication in Abraham's work. But if there had been a genuine hurry to bring a real offense to the attention of the profession, those concerned could have contacted the appropriate AHA division; they could have put something in the AHA newsletter, which has a shorter lead time than the *Review*. The obligation in a case like this is to use the formal communication mechanisms of the profession. There's no evidence that Feldman even considered these possibilities. His method was calculated not to inform, but to intimidate."[15]

In response to those charges, Feldman published an eighteen-page attack in the journal *Central European History*. He wrote that Abraham's "egregious errors, tendentious misconstruals and outright inventions" made the book a "menace to other scholars."[16] He refused to "dignify" Abraham's book with a discussion of its thesis. However, of the errors he attributed to Abraham, none was as serious as the misdated and misattributed document that had already been discussed in the *American Historical Review*.

In a sixty-six-page reply in the same issue, Abraham apologized for his errors, which he termed "inexcusable."[17] He distinguished the minor from the major ones; he argued convincingly that he neither fabricated documents nor systematically misconstrued them; and he pointed out a couple of errors in Feldman's critique. Feldman followed with a thirty-four-page rejoinder, terming Abraham's reply "an insult to our profession." As for his own errors, he wrote, "I have decided to forgive myself."[18] Beneath the rhetorical smoke, Feldman quietly abandoned several of his most serious charges, including fraud and forgery, without admitting he had been wrong.

Abraham's critics also said that his "misinformation" began with the dedication in the book: "For my parents, who at Auschwitz and elsewhere suffered the worst consequences of what I can only write about."[19] His detractors pointed out that his mother, although imprisoned at Auschwitz, survived—and thus did not experience "the worst consequences." The best response to this argument is Arno Mayer's question: "Have you no shame?"

Many younger scholars saw the vendetta against Abraham as a consequence of his Marxism, but it was more complicated than that. If Abraham had written a Marxist study of Weimar that didn't discuss the role of businessmen, Henry Turner wouldn't have bothered to check his footnotes. If he had written a Marxist theoretical essay on the Weimar state that didn't present archival evidence, Turner wouldn't have been interested. What aroused Abraham's critics was his having placed his empirical research on the politics of big business within a framework of Marxist theory.

Turner's book, *German Big Business and the Rise of Hitler,* was finally published in 1985 by Oxford University Press; in the *New York Review,* it was reviewed alongside David Abraham's book, which must have made Turner apoplectic.[20] Turner concluded his book with a diatribe against Marxist historians. He didn't distinguish between the neo-Marxists found in American universities and Soviet or East German historians. All sought "to discredit and undermine societies with capitalist economies and to legitimize repressive anti-capitalist regimes."[21] Feldman, on the other hand, denied that he opposed Abraham because he was a Marxist. He did recommend Abraham's book for publication, and before this episode, he had directed dissertations by students on the left.

Abraham's critics focused their outrage almost exclusively on his research concerning the relationship between big businessmen and Hitler. In doing so, they missed the point of the book. It was not an analysis of the growth of Nazism, but a structuralist study of the success and failure of capitalist democracy: how German elites won popular support from socialist and Catholic organized labor, and how this accord failed in the face of the Depression. "The collapse of the Republic and the Nazi assumption of power were by no means the same," Abraham wrote in his conclusion. "That no stable ruling bloc could be organized under a democratic form of state did not, of itself, indicate that a fascist solution, whatever its nature, would follow."[22] The fact that he focused his research on structures rather than individuals was widely praised in reviews and was the basis for the Princeton history department's decision to hire and then promote him.

The vituperative and wide-ranging attack on Abraham's book was, in fact, part of a larger debate between two kinds of historians—those who sought to identify broad levels of causation and those who confined themselves to a chronicle of events. The former group included Marxists as well as structuralists, members of the *Annales* School, and practitioners of cliometrics, all of whom sought to identify general causes beyond the acts and motives of individuals. As for the latter group: "Their attitude," Schorske told me at the time, "is that, because their footnotes don't contain errors, their understanding of history is correct."[23]

The rise of different schools of historical interpretation signaled the decline of a monolithic profession presided over by an establishment of old boys. In the mid-sixties, if the senior men at Yale and Berkeley said an assistant professor was no good, that would have been the end of the matter. The fact that three departments were interested in hiring Abraham in 1984, despite the opinion of two senior men, and that one actually voted to hire him, helps a little to explain Feldman's frenzy.

Abraham wanted Princeton University Press to publish a revised edition of his book in which he would correct the errors. Feldman argued there would be nothing left of the book. Schorske disagreed: "The defects in David's book are glaring and inexcusable," he told me, "but they are without any substantial impact on the unfolding economic and political analysis. When all the errors are corrected, the argument will stand exactly; the historical configuration will not change; the interpretive logic of the book will be upheld."

The Abraham controversy became a prototypical media spectacle. It was reported on page one of the *New York Times* and in *Time*. [24] Feldman told me that "people admire my courage in pursuing this matter," and he was emboldened by that to call for a broadened effort to "clean up shop" in the history profession. Robert Tignor, chair of the Princeton history department at the time, took a different view of the consequences of the case. He told me at the time that he worried about its effect on young scholars: "The message is: don't tread on the toes of established historians. Stay away from controversy. Don't take chances. The history profession is a sea full of sharks." [25]

But it's also full of decent people who came to Abraham's defense. Carl Schorske explained, "David Abraham is a guy who understands historical processes and has a subtle and refined interpretation. That's the reason why one wants to save him for the profession." [26]

Nevertheless, Feldman's campaign succeeded; nobody would hire David Abraham. Princeton University Press decided not to publish a revised and corrected edition of his book, but in 1986, the publisher Holmes & Meier did. Abraham decided to start over, and enrolled in law school at the University of Pennsylvania. In 1991, he was appointed Associate Professor of Law at the University of Miami, where he continues to teach today as a professor of American immigration law. In summer 2000, David Abraham was back in the news: when Cuban-American leaders in Miami tried to block the return of young Elian Gonzalez to his father in Cuba, the *New York Times* quoted David Abraham regularly as their leading expert on immigration law.[27] The Lexis-Nexis news database lists 174 articles about Elian Gonzalez in which University of Miami law professor David Abraham was quoted. And the Holmes & Meier second edition of *Collapse of the Weimar Republic* is still in print.

6
Mike Davis and Power in Los Angeles

What happens to a leading Marxist writer after he gets a MacArthur "genius" grant and a Getty fellowship, and his new book hits number one on the nonfiction bestseller list?[1] If the writer is Mike Davis and the book is *Ecology of Fear,* what happens is that the *New York Times,* the *Economist,* the *Los Angeles Times,* and a variety of other publications large and small take tremendous interest in opponents who zero in on a few errors in the footnotes, manufacture other mistakes, and denounce the book as "fiction" and the author as a "fraud." It was the quintessential media spectacle.

Ecology of Fear got many strong reviews, from the *New York Times Book Review* to *Business Week,* which called it "compelling" and "persuasive."[2] But the attacks, which began in October 1998, were vicious. On its front page, the *Los Angeles Times* quoted critics who described Davis's book as "self-promoting, city-trashing rot"; the *New York Times* quoted critics who declared that there was "something pathological" about the way Davis had "twisted the facts"; and the normally staid *Economist* quoted a columnist calling Davis's work "fake, phoney, made-up, crackpot, bullshit."[3] *Salon,* the on-line magazine, published three attacks on Davis; *New Times LA,* a free weekly, published four; *Suck,* the webzine of *Wired* magazine, published two; and there were more.[4]

Beginning with his first book on Los Angeles, *City of Quartz* (1990), Davis has been a passionate historian and analyst of the underside of a city built on PR and mythologized from its inception as a kind of dreamwork in the desert. Although it was widely praised, *City of Quartz* never made the bestseller list and never aroused much criticism. But after *Ecology of Fear* spent seventeen weeks on the bestseller list, the voices of the Los Angeles establishment, whose policies Davis has excoriated for years, struck back with a vengeance. At heart, it was a battle over who gets to define Los Angeles: the downtown boosters and their journalistic friends, deeply invested in selling the city as a sunny paradise, or Davis, who argued that developers have placed the city at risk of social and environmental disaster, a disaster "as avoidable, as unnatural, as the beating of Rodney King and the ensuing explosion in the streets."[5] Davis's critics were not out to refute his arguments; instead, they sought to destroy him.

The attacks began in a small throwaway weekly in Los Angeles, the *Downtown News,* which published an article by a former development executive named David Friedman reporting on the work of one Brady Westwater, who had set up a twenty-two-page website claiming to document factual errors in Davis's book.[6] That website and associated e-mail to journalists provided the starting point for virtually all of Davis's critics. Westwater opened his manifesto with a critique of the biographical information on the back of *Ecology of Fear,* which said Davis was "born in Los Angeles" when in fact he had been born in Fontana. Fontana is an industrial suburb about twelve miles east of the county line and is generally considered to be part of greater Los Angeles. Davis had hardly kept his birthplace a secret, devoting the final chapter of *City of Quartz* to Fontana's decline since his birth. For Westwater, though, the flap copy was "much like the Stalinist era creation of non-persons," transforming Fontana into a "non-place." To "claim he is a native son with specific firsthand knowledge of LA," Westwater concluded, "is . . . well, fraud."[7]

Anywhere else, such a denunciation would be dismissed as loony, but Westwater's "fraud" charge was repeated over and over, even providing the headline for the *Economist* story.

The *New York Times* devoted three paragraphs to Westwater's charge that Davis was "lying" when he argued that L.A.'s good-weather ideology had led to media amnesia about the existence of tornadoes in the region. The *Times* story then had Davis replying that all books contain errors and "the thing you have to understand about these books is I'm a socialist." In fact, Davis's documentation of the absence of the word "tornado" in *Los Angeles Times* headlines was systematic and convincing, and in an interview Davis denied he ever implied that his being a socialist was an explanation for alleged errors about tornadoes.[8]

Besides regurgitating Westwater, virtually all of the critics focused on three sentences in an *LA Weekly* cover story on Davis written by Lewis MacAdams. That piece praised Davis's book as a far-sighted analysis probing the links between "social injustice and eco-logical distress."[9] MacAdams also recounted his first meeting with Davis, ten years previously, when Davis was interviewing him for a story for the *Weekly*. MacAdams wrote that Davis showed him a draft of the interview, which described the two conversing "at the Fremont Gate entrance to Elysian Park, a place I'd never been," and which attributed quotes to MacAdams that "made me sound like I knew a lot more . . . than I actually did." MacAdams told me he didn't regard this as a problem, and, as he also wrote in the *Weekly*, "I told him to go ahead with the piece just the way it was."[10] MacAdams rightly insisted that this was not the same thing as making up characters or stories. Sue Horton, editor at the time of *LA Weekly*, said in an interview, "What Mike did was wrong. He shouldn't have done it." Davis said the same thing: "Yeah, it was a mistake."[11]

But Horton also pointed out that "a lot of *Ecology of Fear* first appeared in Mike's column for *LA Weekly* in '96 or '97. I edited it for the more than a year that it ran. We fact-checked it every week. There was never anything in that column that didn't check."[12]

After *New Times LA* published its first attack, Horton said, "We fact-checked a couple of the 'errors' they cited, just for sport. We took Mike's statement that the '94 Northridge earthquake was the most expensive disaster in American history and had a fact-checker start cold on that. He talked to a disaster research center in Colorado. They said yes, indisputably, the most expensive disaster in American history was the '94 Northridge earthquake."[13]

As with any 484-page book with 831 footnotes, *Ecology of Fear* contains some mistakes. This is an inescapable pitfall of publishing.

No one accuses the *New York Times,* America's newspaper of record, of "fraud" because every day it runs a "Corrections" column. In 1998, the year *Ecology of Fear* was published, the *Times* ran 2,130 corrections, an average of six per day. As it turns out, the errors in *Ecology of Fear* that were so exciting Davis's opponents were either trivial or based on misunderstanding. For example, Veronique de Turenne complained in *Salon* that, while Davis said there are 2,000 gangs in Los Angeles, in fact there were only 1,850.[14] When I asked Davis about the discrepancy, he said, "The missing gangs are in Orange County. She's talking about L.A. County, while I was talking about the Census Bureau's Los Angeles Standard Metropolitan Statistical District, which includes Orange County."[15] But even if de Turenne were right, should Angelenos feel better about the social health of their city because it had a mere 1,850 gangs?

Who were these people, and why were they saying those terrible things about Mike Davis? David Friedman, who wrote the first story attacking Davis, had been president of Catellus Resources Group, part of the Catellus Development Corporation, a billion-dollar real estate company that at the time operated or leased 20 million square feet of income-producing buildings, mostly in California. Friedman resigned in 1998 to "pursue personal print and broadcast media opportunities," he said in a press release at the time. The company assured its stockholders that, although Friedman had been "named a contributing editor to the *Los Angeles Times* Opinion section and a contributor to *Inc. Magazine,*" he would continue to work "as a consultant following his departure."[16]

Joel Kotkin, often cited as "an urban policy expert" in articles criticizing Davis's footnotes, described himself to the *New York Times* as "a person who was trained as a Marxist" angry that Davis has "bastardize[d] Marxist theory."[17] In fact he was a research fellow at the Reason Foundation, a right-wing libertarian think tank, as well as a senior fellow at the conservative Pepperdine Institute for Public Policy.[18] Kotkin's political differences with Davis were evident in his article in *American Enterprise* magazine arguing that "an increasingly left-wing AFL-CIO" was "bringing class-warfare politics" to Los Angeles. President John Sweeney, he wrote, had "opened the AFL-CIO to participation by delegates openly linked to the Communist Party, which enthusiastically backed his ascent." The heirs of "the totalitarian left," he concluded, were threatening the city of Los Angeles. Among the leaders of this menacing camp: Mike Davis.[19] Kotkin is a frequent co-author with Friedman; their pieces on the "new L.A. economy," extolling sweatshops as examples of immigrant entrepreneurialism, have appeared on op-ed pages in the *Washington Post* and *Los Angeles Times*.[20]

Brady Westwater, upon whose efforts as a "fact checker" both Kotkin and Friedman relied, is a pseudonym for Ross Ernest Shockley, a Malibu realtor who no doubt was troubled by Davis's chapter "The Case for Letting Malibu Burn." It is a compelling indictment of the systematic neglect of fire dangers faced by poor inner-city Angelenos, contrasted with the waste of public resources providing fire protection for scattered mansions in remote areas of Malibu, where brush fires in the dry season are inevitable. The *New York Times* did not mention Westwater's interest here and promoted him to the rank of "amateur local historian."[21] Until Friedman publicized the efforts of Westwater, none of the dozens of journalists who received the latter's nutty report would go near it.

The *Los Angeles Times* occupies a special place among Davis's critics. As Davis detailed in *City of Quartz,* the paper's owners in the first part of the twentieth century were major players in creating Los Angeles, joining in "syndicates to monopolize the subdivision of Hollywood, the San Fernando Valley and much of northeastern LA."[22] The *Times* has never wavered from its commitment to regional development and boosterism. A few years before *Ecology of Fear,* Davis contributed some opinion pieces to the paper, and the book got a mixed review in the paper.[23] But the paper's article on *Ecology of Fear* had a revealing subtext: Davis was too "gloomy" to be "the pre-eminent analyst of L.A.'s soul." It objected in particular to his description of Los Angeles as a place "where the future has turned rancid."[24] The *Economist* made a similar argument: Davis's success "lies in the fact that the New York publishing establishment has a weakness for books that portray the upstart city of the West, its chief cultural rival, in the worst possible light."[25]

The issue that lay beneath the surface was: who is allowed to portray Los Angeles? The *Times* and the downtown developers preferred Kevin Starr, the state librarian and upbeat historian of California, who was quoted more than once recommending that Davis "wake up" and "smell the roses."[26] The *Economist* complained that Davis neglected the city's "flowering of public spaces," while the *Downtown News* criticized him for failing to praise the city's economic recovery after the military cutbacks of the early nineties.[27]

It's not unfair to call Mike Davis's work "dark," and for those who live on the sunny side of the street in Southern California, the boosters' picture may be an accurate depiction of their own experience. But as Davis reminded me, 4 million Latinos now live in Los Angeles, and they didn't come for the sun. The State of California was spending more than $5 billion a year on prisons, and Los Angeles County at the time had 725,000 people on welfare.[28] Davis never denies that L.A.'s winners have indeed won very big. It was his presentation of the experience of the rest of the city's people that the boosters sought to erase.

At least one of Davis's critics admitted that his portrayal of Los Angeles was accurate. Of *Salon*'s three attacks on the book, one was written by D.J. Waldie, the author of *Holy Land,* a wonderful book on the Los Angeles suburb of Lakewood. Although Waldie disliked *Ecology of Fear* intensely, he agreed that its most important claims about Los Angeles were true: it was indeed "the most segregated big city in the nation" from 1900 to 1970; it did have "the most destructive civil disturbances in the nation's modern history" in 1965 and 1992; "L.A.'s social landscape was deliberately made a mechanism for sorting communities by race, class and income more rigorously than in any other American big city"; Davis's "criticisms of hillside development in Malibu [and] earthquake failure downtown . . . are true." Waldie rejected the book only because it was "so hopeless" about the prospects for improvement and reform.[29]

Even if the critics were right that the Los Angeles economy had recovered and its crime rate had dropped over the years preceding the publication of the book, that doesn't disprove the central thesis of *Ecology of Fear,* which is a more original and significant work than its critics acknowledge. (Interest declared: one of my books was published in a series co-edited by Davis, and I am listed in the acknowledgments of *Ecology of Fear*.) The book was far more than a "gloomy" or "hopeless" account of the inequalities of wealth and power in Los Angeles. It looked at the city in terms of its long environmental history—history measured not in decades or centuries but in thousands of years. Davis was bringing to a broad public the findings of scientists who have concluded that, for the past few hundred years, Los Angeles has been in a relatively quiet period of earthquake activity (a "seismic siesta"), as well as a relatively wet one in terms of rainfall. Scientists are concerned that the long-term pattern suggests much bigger and more frequent earthquakes in the future, as well as much longer and more devastating periods of drought—lasting possibly for decades.

Davis's critics avoided those fundamental arguments, and it's not hard to see why. "For a nonscientist, Davis has done an excellent job of synthesizing the state of the field," Lisa Grant, who teaches earthquake science at the University of California, Irvine, told me. "I was impressed by his chapter [on earthquakes]. He has the right sources, and I didn't find any inaccuracies in the footnotes."[30] Richard Walker, chairman of the geography department at UC Berkeley, agreed: "Most of what Mike is saying is completely accepted wisdom among scholars who work in the area of environmental hazards. . . . Extreme events, so-called natural disasters, are predictable, inevitable and inevitably made worse by human activity. The character of human activity is absolutely critical to the human losses."[31]

A responsible society would address environmental dangers, Davis argued. Yet the people who controlled the development of Los Angeles were ignoring them. By promoting high-rise, high-density development, they were creating the potential for immense harm to the millions of ordinary working people who lived in the city. *Ecology of Fear* was intended as part of a dialogue between social justice advocates and environmentalists, and as an undisguised polemic arguing that the city should abandon its reckless pattern of development. The way Davis made that argument was his real contribution. But on every one of those issues so vital to the city's future, his critics were strangely silent.

The media spectacle worked, but only in the short run. The attacks succeeded in driving Mike Davis out of Los Angeles. The year of the attacks on *Ecology of Fear,* the history departments at both USC and UCLA were searching for senior scholars in the history of California and/or the West. Davis applied to both, but neither department so much as short-listed him. Maybe that's because they didn't like his work, but maybe it's because the *Los Angeles Times* was running articles on page one about charges of research fraud in his book.

He ended up leaving Los Angeles and moving to the east coast for a job in the history department at SUNY-Stony Brook. Evidently, the search committee and administration there concluded that the errors in his footnotes were minor and that he met the requirements for appointment to a tenured position.

He returned to Southern California, and a tenured position in the history department at the University of California, Irvine, four years later, but only after publishing a massive new scholarly book on a different topic: *Late Victorian Holocausts: El Niño Famines and the Making of the Third World.* That book was praised in the *New York Times Book Review* by Amartya Sen, who had won the Nobel Prize in Economics. Davis's new book also won the prize of the World

History Association for the best book of the year. "Davis's range is stunning," wrote Kenneth Pomeranz, president of the World History Assocation at the time and chair of the department at Irvine when Davis was hired. "He combines political economy, meteorology, and ecology with vivid narratives to create a book that is both a gripping read and a major conceptual achievement. Lots of us talk about writing 'world history' and 'inter-disciplinary history': here is the genuine article."[32]

The Mike Davis case shows how a lone nut with a website can initiate a media spectacle and do considerable damage—if the figure he's attacking has powerful enemies. It also shows how at least some universities can evaluate work that is the focus of a media spectacle and come to an appropriate conclusion. So the case of Mike Davis has a happy ending—despite the campaign to discredit him, the author of several good books got a good job.

One key difference between the Mike Davis case and those of Michael Bellesiles and David Abraham is that the attacks on Davis did not come from professional historians or other academics.[33] No scholarly journals ever ran debates about charges of fraud in his work, and no universities appointed special committees to investigate him. And the power arrayed against him—the *Los Angeles Times*—itself underwent a change of editors; the editorial team that had targeted him was replaced by the paper's new owners, and the new people didn't seem to know or care about their predecessors' campaign. When the *Los Angeles Times* returned to write about Mike Davis in 2004, the coverage was completely benign.[34]

III

Misconduct Without Media Spectacle

7

The Denmark Vesey "Trial Record": A New Verdict

The record for the largest number of errors in a work of history on a significant topic probably goes to Edward Pearson for his 1999 book purporting to reproduce the trial transcript of Denmark Vesey, a slave accused of plotting insurrection in South Carolina in 1821.[1] The volume was shown to be riddled with errors from beginning to end—thousands of errors,[2] so many that correction was impossible; the publisher had to withdraw the book from publication. Pearson declared in print that he "pled guilty" to publishing a work that was "deeply flawed" by his "unrelenting carelessness." He conceded that the evidence of his errors was "overwhelming," and agreed that the "historical community" needed to be alerted to the "unreliability" of his work. He concluded, "I openly admit to these mistakes for which I take sole responsibility and for which I unreservedly apologize."[3]

The errors were not only pervasive; they were also significant—so significant that the historian who discovered them, Michael P. Johnson of Johns Hopkins University, came to the opposite conclusion from Pearson's about the events in question: Johnson concluded that Vesey was not a rebel leader but rather an innocent man who had been framed. His article exposing the errors in the Pearson volume and arguing a new interpretation of the Vesey case won the ABC-CLIO prize, awarded by the Organization of American Historians for the best article of the year in all of American history.

It's hard to think of another case involving an important historical issue—like slave rebellion—in which an historian committed errors on such a massive scale. Nevertheless, these problems were ignored by the media, and Edward Pearson suffered no disciplinary action from his college, Franklin and Marshall, where the provost decided none was appropriate. Thus despite the severe problems with his book, Pearson continued to serve as chair of the department there.[4] The case of the Denmark Vesey "Trial Record" thus raises the question, when do historians' errors get overlooked or forgiven?

Denmark Vesey has been celebrated as the leader of one of America's small number of slave insurrections. He was a free black carpenter in Charleston who was executed in 1822, charged with organizing South Carolina slaves to rise up. The plot described in court included setting fire to the city of Charleston, killing all the white people, and seizing ships in the harbor and sailing to Haiti (at the time, the only free black republic in the world). It would have been the biggest slave rebellion in our history, historians say, but Vesey and his comrades were betrayed by an informer.

In a stunning piece of historical detective work, which appeared in the *William and Mary Quarterly,* the most prestigious journal of early American history, in 2001, Johnson reported the errors in the Pearson volume, revisited the archives to examine the original documents, and concluded that Vesey was innocent—that he did not plot a slave uprising, but instead had been framed. The politically ambitious mayor of Charleston, Johnson argued, used the alleged plot to discredit his political rival, the state's governor, and advance his own career by claiming to rescue South Carolina from an uprising that the governor's own slaves were planning to join.

Johnson started out with an assignment to review Pearson's edited volume *Designs against Charleston: The Trial Record of the Denmark Vesey Slave Conspiracy of 1822.* The book had been acclaimed by leading historians of slavery. Ira Berlin, at the time president of the Organization of American Historians, wrote a pre-publication blurb calling the Pearson transcript "a document of signal importance in the study of American history," and saying "Edward Pearson has edited it with intelligence and care." Drew Gilpin Faust of the University of Pennsylvania wrote in her blurb, "This volume is a wonderful resource for teaching, but represents as well an important scholarly contribution in its own right."[5]

The published reviews that preceded Johnson's were equally laudatory. In the official journal of the Organization of American Historians, the *Journal of American History,* reviewer Lorri Glover of the University of Tennessee-Knoxville praised the book for an "imaginative blending of analysis and primary documents," "a fascinating look at black resistance" that "enriches scholarly understanding of the Vesey conspiracy."[6] In the *Journal of Southern History,* published by the Southern Historical Assocation, reviewer Barbara L. Bellows of the Institute for Southern Studies at the University of South Carolina described the book as "a careful compilation" that "gives an unprecedented glimpse into the inner world of Charleston's African-Americans." She concluded that "everyone interested in understanding the long tragic story leading to the coming of the Civil War will find the record of the Vesey conspiracy trial riveting reading."[7] And in the *North Carolina Historical Review,* Randall M. Miller of Saint Joseph's University wrote that the Pearson volume contained "one of the fullest records of any slave revolt. It is now possible to view rebellion from the perspective of those who would be free. . . . In their own words, those who imagined their own liberty spoke (and speak) most eloquently."[8] Other reviews were equally full of praise.

Of course no reviewer is expected to consult the primary sources cited in a book under review—the assumption is that the author has fulfilled his duty to accuracy. Johnson went beyond the normal responsibilities of the reviewer, and, because he was doing research in the archive where Pearson had found the original "trial transcript," he was able to compare the original documents to the version Pearson had published.

To understand the seriousness of Pearson's offenses, it's necessary to describe Johnson's findings in some detail. Johnson's report was devastating—perhaps the most devastating account of error ever to appear in a history journal. Johnson reported finding "5,000–6,000 discrepancies" between the "evidence manuscript in the archives and the transcript" published in Pearson's book.[9]

Pearson said two manuscripts of a trial transcript exist, and that one "replicates" the other; but Johnson reported he was completely wrong about this. There are two documents; one is a "brief printed narrative of the trials," not as Pearson had described it, a court transcript. The other document is labeled "Evidence," and seems to be in part a summary written at the end of each day of testimony. That document isn't a true transcript of court proceedings, either, as Pearson claimed; both, Johnson shows, are "revised versions of the words witnesses uttered," revised by persons unknown to us, and thus definitely not verbatim accounts of the testimony of witnesses and the accused. Thus Pearson's volume is not, as his title claims, a "trial transcript."

Pearson's volume is based mostly on the printed narrative, which Johnson shows was written after the "Evidence" document and appears to be a retrospective account.[10] Pearson failed to see the difference between the two documents describing the trial, and relied on the one more distant from the proceedings, which he erroneously described as a "trial transcript."

Even in the document Pearson reprinted, his transcription is riddled with errors. In the first twenty-nine words Pearson published in his edition, Pearson made ten errors—ranging from omitting words to adding punctuation to getting the number of members of the court wrong. Johnson found 550 instances where Pearson's volume added, omitted, or changed words in the original sources. He got the opening date of the trial wrong. He omitted the "not guilty" pleas of five of the accused, and another who pleaded guilty he records as pleading "not guilty."[11]

But these errors paled beside the most significant problem of the Pearson volume. It purported to describe "the trial of Denmark Vesey." But, Johnson shows, there was no trial. "The manuscript transcript contains no mention of a trial. . . . It says nothing about the presence in court of Vesey or . . . his counsel. It says nothing about Vesey facing his accusers or questioning them. . . . Not a single word of testimony from Denmark Vesey exists in the manuscript."[12] What happened was that the court questioned witnesses for the prosecution, then decided Vesey was guilty, and ordered him and others executed.

But Pearson's volume "creates the illusion of trials" and claims to present testimony of the accused. He scrambled the chronology and reorganized the testimony to create the kind of courtroom confrontations modern readers are familiar with. This appears to be the result not of intentional or motivated deception, but rather stems from his reliance on a third document, the published *Official Report*—which was again not a transcript of the trial, but rather a retrospective justification of the proceedings, intended to refute critics. It's "a document of advocacy," Johnson writes, a "retrospective statement of the prosecution's case" which "must be read and interpreted with the suspicion warranted by special pleading."[13] Instead Pearson presented it as a true and accurate transcript.

Thus it's hard to imagine a more flawed and unreliable work than Pearson's "trial transcript." Pearson conceded that all of Johnson's criticisms were legitimate, and he said in extenuation only that his errors were not intentional or motivated but rather the result of "carelessness."[14]

But Johnson didn't end his work with this exhaustive exercise in checking original sources. If what Pearson published as a "trial transcript" was in fact a retrospective statement of the prosecution's case, intended to silence critics, who were these critics and what arguments was the prosecution intending to silence? What really happened in Charleston? Whereas Pearson, along with all other Vesey scholars, describes Vesey as a heroic leader of a planned rebellion that was sold out by informers, Johnson came to a radically different and immensely significant conclusion.

The new evidence for Johnson's revisionist account came from records of court proceedings in Charleston, in which 131 black men were charged. Eventually, thirty-five were executed. Court documents include testimony by thirty-three slaves, who described a bold and bloodthirsty plan that has gone down in history as the Vesey conspiracy. But Johnson argued that all the testimony was coerced by beatings and the threat of execution, and thus none of it should be taken at face value. The choice faced by Vesey and the accused slaves was a terrible one: testify falsely against the other accused men and live, or refuse to testify falsely and die.

Virtually all historians before Johnson relied on the *Official Report* of the trial, published after the court proceedings. The *Official Report* names Vesey "the head of this conspiracy."[15] Johnson instead used the "Evidence" transcript itself, which exists in manuscript in the South Carolina state archives. The court proceedings were held in secret; the public and the press were barred from attendance, so the "Evidence" transcript is the only authoritative contemporary source.

Johnson showed that the "Evidence" transcript is different in crucial respects from the *Official Report,* which describes dramatic scenes where Vesey confronts and questions his accusers and makes statements in his own defense. But the "Evidence" transcript does not contain a single word of testimony from Vesey. There is nothing suggesting Vesey was even present during the proceedings. Most astonishing, the "Evidence" transcript does not even refer to a trial of Denmark Vesey. The transcript indicates that the court (consisting of seven men) questioned witnesses about a conspiracy, and then decided that Vesey and five slaves were guilty. But there was no consensus among the witnesses that Vesey was the head of the plot; at least six witnesses named people other than Vesey as the leader.[16]

Johnson makes a convincing case that the conspiracy in Charleston in 1822 was not a plan by blacks to kill whites, but rather a conspiracy by whites to kill blacks. The result was the largest number of executions ever carried out by a civilian court in the United States.

The larger political context, and the political culture in which the court proceedings took place, are crucial to the new view. Four of the first black men to be arrested and charged with plotting rebellion were the most trusted household slaves of South Carolina Governor Thomas Bennett. He had been active in state politics for almost twenty years and drew on his considerable authority to protest the verdicts. In a report to the legislature, the governor criticized the court for "an usurpation of authority, and a violation of Law." He objected to the secrecy of the trial and in particular to the conviction of defendants on the basis of secret testimony and a refusal to allow the accused to face their accusers. He suggested that the testimony was "the offspring of treachery or revenge, and the hope of immunity."[17]

A second key figure in the slaveholding elite challenged the fairness of the proceedings against Vesey: a U.S. Supreme Court Justice appointed by Thomas Jefferson named William Johnson Jr., the governor's brother-in-law. He published a story in the *Charleston Courier* about a wave of hysteria over a nonexistent slave rebellion a decade earlier that had resulted in the hanging of an innocent slave.[18] The members of the Vesey court were outraged by the jurist's implicit criticism and demanded that he retract the suggestions that they were "capable of committing perjury and murder."[19]

Thus, as Michael Johnson summed up in his *William and Mary Quarterly* article, within a few weeks of the end of the court proceedings that resulted in Vesey's execution, "the members of the court had been criticized in public by a justice of the United States Supreme Court for committing legalized murder and in private by the governor of South Carolina for sending black men to the gallows in proceedings that could not withstand public scrutiny."[20]

The court responded to this criticism of its methods and its sentences by arresting an additional eighty-two suspects, taking more testimony about a planned slave rebellion, and then ordering the execution of twenty-nine more slaves, bringing the total of executions to thirty-five. The message was clear: the court was defending white Charleston against a massive and terrifying conspiracy. Anybody who criticized the proceedings was putting white South Carolina in mortal danger.

James Hamilton Jr. was the politically ambitious mayor of Charleston who had engineered the executions. His claim to have saved white Charleston from a murderous slave conspiracy was, Johnson says, "his path to power."[21] After the executions he was elected to Congress; he served in the House for seven years, then ran for governor and was elected in 1830 as the leader of the "nullification" forces, those who argued that states had the right to declare null and void any federal law they considered unconstitutional. Nullification helped launch South Carolina on the path to secession thirty years later. (Hamilton was killed in a steamboat accident in 1857, four years before South Carolina led the South to war.)

The future of slavery was a hot political issue in Charleston in 1822. The trial and executions deepened a growing sense of crisis for the slaveholding elite of the city and state. The elite were already dividing between a more paternalistic group, of which the governor was a prime example, and others seeking a more militant defense of the system from its enemies in the North. In Washington, Congress had passed the Missouri Compromise two years earlier, establishing its right to prohibit slavery in federal territory. The Missouri crisis worried slaveowners about the growing power of antislavery sentiment in the North. In South Carolina, the legislature had recently made it illegal for masters to free their slaves, and the legislature was faced with a number of petitions and bills sponsored by particular slaveholders seeking freedom for particular slaves. Supreme Court Justice William Johnson worried that slaveowner hysteria was heading toward secession as early as 1823, after Vesey and the others were hanged, when he wrote in a letter to Thomas Jefferson, "I fear nothing so much as the Effects of the persecuting Spirit that is abroad in this Place [Charleston]. Should it spread thro' the State & produce a systematic Policy founded on the ridiculous but prevalent Notion—that it is a struggle for Life or Death, [then] there are no Excesses that we may not look for—whatever be their Effect upon the Union."[22]

The new view of Denmark Vesey raises a larger question about slavery. The Vesey rebellion conspiracy has been seen as one of a handful of examples of militant, coordinated, large-scale resistance in a country where slaves almost never rebelled. Vesey's boldness and bravery have been honored for decades. But if Vesey was simply an innocent victim, must we conclude that South Carolina slaves in 1822 failed to resist slavery?

Johnson suggested that the true story contains a different kind of heroism: the heroism of Vesey and the other forty-four men who pleaded not guilty and refused to testify falsely against fellow slaves—who made the terrible choice to face execution for telling the truth rather than send others to the gallows on the basis of a lie. Indeed, 83 percent of the men arrested refused to testify falsely; despite extensive torture, 90 percent of the incriminating testimony in the deadliest phase of the trials came from only six slaves. Johnson concludes: "It is time to pay attention to the 'not guilty' pleas of almost all the men who went to the gallows," to honor them for "their refusal to name names in order to save themselves."[23]

There were also some heroes in white Charleston: eventually twenty-seven white Charlestonians testified in court in support of fifteen black defendants. Their message was that whites should tell the truth and resist hysteria.

Johnson's new interpretation is not accepted by all the experts. In a subsequent issue of the *William and Mary Quarterly,* three authors who celebrated Vesey as a rebel hero argued that the court's use of beatings and death threats did not mean the testimony they obtained was necessarily false. The three were Douglas Egerton of Le Moyne College, author of a 1999 book on Vesey; David Robertson, a novelist, poet, and librarian in Cincinnati who also wrote a Vesey biography that year; and Edward Pearson, editor of the discredited "Trial Transcript." The three Vesey biographers were joined by Robert Paquette of Hamilton College, a historian of slave conspiracy in the Caribbean.[24] The four argued in different ways that witnesses for the prosecution told the truth to save their own skins. None of the four convincingly explained the "not guilty" pleas of the others, or the criticism from whites of the methods and conclusions of the court.

Four other historians of slavery wrote in the *Quarterly* that Johnson had convinced them to change their minds about the Vesey conspiracy. Winthrop Jordan, Distinguished Professor of History and Afro-American Studies at the University of Mississippi and author of several prizewinning histories of slavery, including the now-classic *White Over Black,* commented, "Well, there goes another firm fact of life." He suggested that "we need to stop requiring slaves to have behaved in ways that we now think would have been heroic."[25]

Philip Morgan, another prizewinning historian of slavery, former editor of the *William and Mary Quarterly,* and professor at Johns Hopkins, wrote, "The truly daunting aspect of Michael P. Johnson's extraordinary tour de force . . . is the complicity of historians in accepting the corrupt verdict of a kangaroo court." What should we conclude from this? Historians, Morgan wrote, have "a natural tendency to highlight 'freedom fighters,' as if entitlement to human dignity depended on a readiness to engage in violent struggle. The assumption is that only through a willingness to sacrifice life could slaves prove their worthiness for emancipation."[26]

Several other prominent historians commented on the controversy, including Drew Gilpin Faust, now dean of the Radcliffe Institute for Advanced Study at Harvard University: "I have problems with finding heroism as the purpose of history," she told me. "I've always written about people so far from being heroes. I'm interested in the complexity of people's lives, so the loss of a rebel hero doesn't bother me."[27]

The new view of Denmark Vesey undermines what had been seen as a rich source of insight into slave consciousness and culture—the testimony of the witnesses who confessed. Slaves left few written records, and the lengthy statements in the *Official Report* attributed to dozens of slaves have often been quoted and cited by historians of black culture. In his comment on Johnson in the *William and Mary Quarterly,* James Sidbury wrote that we should see that "the seemingly rich window that the trial records open on enslaved Americans' desire for freedom is actually a mirror reflecting white paranoia."[28]

Other historians argued that Johnson did not disprove the story of Vesey as a rebel. Peter Wood, award-winning historian of slavery at Duke, told me, "You can have both sides of this story. Just because you have white paranoia doesn't mean you don't also have black people with a strong will to resist. What has happened in the last thirty years is we've tended to give more attention to the will to resist and less than we should have to the machinations of the white power structure."[29]

Meanwhile in Charleston, a long fight by black activists finally succeeded in 2000 in persuading the city to approve a monument honoring Denmark Vesey as a slave rebel leader. Originally, opposition to the monument came mainly from a group of local whites, who protested that Vesey had planned "genocide" for the city's white people. A conference was held in honor of the monument project. Johnson presented his evidence that Vesey was innocent of the charges and more likely one of scores of black victims of a conspiracy engineered by the white power structure. At the conference Johnson was asked whether he thought the city should construct a monument. He said it should, not because Vesey was an insurrectionist but because "he evidently believed that slavery was wrong and that blacks should be equal to whites," and because he was the victim of a "vicious legalized murder."[30] And since the City of Charleston was the official body that organized the court that tried and executed the black men, Johnson said, the city should sponsor the monument. The last report in the *Post and Courier* said that "the Memorial is now planned for Hampton Park and is in the fundraising stage."[31]

Meanwhile, as a result of Johnson's award-winning rethinking of the case, the textbooks are beginning to shift their presentation of Denmark Vesey. One of the newest—with Peter Wood as an author—says "the historical record strongly suggests that no [slave uprising] plot ever existed. Black 'witnesses' who feared for their own lives provided inconsistent and contradictory testimony to a panel of judges. . . . Under fire from other Charleston elites for rushing to judgment, the judges redoubled their efforts to embellish vague rumors of black discontent into a tale of a well-orchestrated uprising. . . . Of those executed, Vesey and 23 other men said nothing to support even the vaguest charges of the court." This textbook concludes that the Vesey case tells us more about "white's fears about free men of color" than it does about black people.[32]

The story of the Denmark Vesey "trial record" is thus a subject of some public interest, which raises anew the question of why Pearson's errors received so little attention outside the *William and Mary Quarterly.* Only one newspaper reported on the controversy—the *New York Times* ran a story by Dinitia Smith on its Saturday "Arts and Ideas" page.[33] Pearson did have his book withdrawn from publication. But unlike other recent cases where historians were charged with varieties of misconduct in their research, Pearson was not subject to investigation by the professional assocations. The official journal, the *Journal of American History* (*JAH*), had published a glowing review of the book; subsequently the journal never even noted that the publisher had withdrawn the volume after it was shown to be unreliable. (The *Journal of Southern History,* in contrast, published a statement in its November 2003 issue that the University of North Carolina Press had withdrawn the book; the editor also invited their reviewer to publish a reconsideration.)[34]

At Pearson's college, Franklin and Marshall, the provost, C. Bruce Pipes, explained the procedures he followed. "Once I became aware of concerns about Ted's monograph that were raised in the literature," he told me in an e-mail, "I called Ted in and heard his version of the story." Then he asked a dean to report to him on the book and the published criticisms of it. "He gave me a very detailed report and in the summary findings he noted that there had been no public or private allegations of professional misconduct against Ted." The provost informed Pearson of the dean's findings, "and told him I would take the report to our Professional Standards Committee (i.e. our tenure and promotions committee) for its advice." The committee's advice was confidential; Pipes told me "I took final action that comprised a sanction, but no disciplinary action." The nature of the sanction also remains confidential.

As for Pearson's continuing as chair of the History Department, that was "handled by our normal procedure of soliciting the opinions from all members of the departmental faculty, taking a recommendation to the Professional Standards Committee, and acting on the committee's advice."[35] Thus Franklin and Marshall's procedures seem thorough and reasonable.

The *JAH* didn't do as well. Its editors should have published a note in its book review section about the book being withdrawn. But the resolution of the problem by other journals, the University of North Carolina Press, and Frankin and Marshall College was appropriate. The profession was informed of the fatal problems in the book by the leading journal in the field; the author was given a chance to respond, which he did; his publisher withdrew the book; and the college decided after due deliberation that no additional action on their part was necessary. That was the end of the case. Errors were corrected, an unreliable publication was removed, the significance of the errors was debated—with fruitful results for the field.

But there is a reason why that's where the story ends: unlike the Bellesiles case, there is no organized constituency campaigning to reconsider the historical role of Denmark Vesey. Indeed, the constituency that exists wants to preserve his memory as a rebel leader rather than an innocent victim. Thus nobody used the Internet to organize a campaign to demand that Franklin and Marshall investigate and punish the historian whose work contained errors; no website beat the drums to raise the level of outrage; college administrators and trustees were not made targets of letter-writing campaigns. In the absence of organized pressure, the profession (with the exception of the *JAH*) and the college did their work with fairness and came to an appropriate conclusion.

8

John Lott, Gun Rights, and Research Fraud

The book has been called "the bible of the gun lobby": *More Guns, Less Crime* by John R. Lott Jr., published in 1998 by the prestigious University of Chicago Press. It has sold 100,000 copies and presents what purports to be statistical evidence showing that states that permit citizens to carry guns have lower crime rates. The book has been the key document in persuading states to pass what are called "concealed carry" gun laws—laws requiring authorities to issue a permit to carry concealed weapons to any qualified applicant who requests one. Thirty-five states have done so—most recently Minnesota, where Lott's arguments provided key ammunition for Republican gun advocates.[1] "Were Lott to be discredited," Chris Mooney wrote in *Mother Jones,* "an entire branch of pro-gun advocacy could lose its chief social scientific basis."[2]

Gun control advocates had presented strong evidence that most guns in the home are used on family members rather than intruders; Lott needed to refute that argument. His case rests entirely on statistics, and at the beginning of the book, Lott gives readers one of his strongest statistics: "98 per cent of the time that people use guns defensively, they merely have to brandish a weapon to break off an attack."[3] You didn't have to shoot a gun to fend off a criminal; merely displaying it did the trick. That 98 percent was an astounding figure—and one that now seems fraudulent. Yet the mainstream media, which showed so much dedication to charges that Michael Bellesiles's research was fraudulent, showed almost no interest in similar charges against Lott.

The first edition of the Lott book, published in May 1998, gave the vaguest possible source for the 98 percent figure: "national surveys."[4] Lott had given a more specific source in a *Wall Street Journal* opinion piece published in July 1997: "Other research shows that guns clearly deter criminals. Polls by the *Los Angeles Times,* Gallup and Peter Hart Research Associates show that there are at least 760,000, and possibly as many as 3.6 million, defensive uses of guns per year. In 98 per cent of the cases, such polls show, people simply brandish the weapon to stop an attack." That was untrue—none of those polls showed what he claimed they did. But he repeated that statement in op-ed pieces published in the *Chicago Tribune,* the *Los Angeles Times,* the *Chicago Sun-Times,* the *Dallas Morning News,* and in testimony before the House Judiciary Committee.[5]

Then critics began to question Lott's figure. In the lead was Otis Dudley Duncan, a retired sociologist at the University of California,

Santa Barbara, who first raised questions in the January 2000 issue of *The Criminologist.*[6] In response to the critics, when the second edition of Lott's book was published later in 2000, Lott cited a completely different and new source: "a national survey I conducted."[7] For three years before this, Lott had never mentioned a national survey he conducted—he had always said the 98 percent figure came from other people's surveys.

At this point, James Lindgren, the Northwestern University law professor who had done an immense amount of work checking Bellesiles's footnotes, decided to take up the issue after reading critiques from Duncan and Tim Lambert, director of the Program in Computer Science at the University of New South Wales (who now maintains a website devoted to the Lott case).[8] When Lindgren asked Lott about the national survey Lott claimed to have done, Lott told him that he lost all the data—on 2,424 people—in a computer crash.[9]

Lindgren saw this claim for what it was: "all evidence of a study with 2,400 respondents does not just disappear when a computer crashes," he wrote on his website in September 2001.

Having done one large survey (about half the size of John Lott's) and several smaller surveys, I can attest that it is an enormous undertaking. Typically, there is funding, employees who did the survey, financial records on the employees, financial records on the mailing or telephoning, the survey instrument, completed surveys or tally sheets, a list of everyone in the sample, records on who responded and who declined to participate, and so on. While not all of these things might be preserved in every study, some of them would usually be retained or recoverable. Just to get a representative list of the US public would take consultation with an experienced sampler and probably the purchase of an expensive sample. As far as I know, there was no cheap commercial list of almost every person or household in the United States from which to draw a good sample.[10]

But John Lott had none of this: no funding, no records of employees or phone calls, no tally sheets, no consultants, nothing. He told Lindgren the phone calls had been made by undergraduate volunteers who he had not paid. He said he couldn't remember the names of any of them. He said he had no phone records because the student volunteers called from their own phones. He said he reimbursed them out of his own pocket for the phone calls they made, but kept no record of his expenses. He didn't have a copy of his survey instrument and didn't remember the wording of the questions. As for the sample, he told Lindgren he drew it off a CD-ROM, but he didn't have the CD-ROM and didn't remember where he got it.

In a last-ditch attempt to come up with evidence that the survey had indeed been conducted, Lindgren suggested e-mailing all former students who might have worked on it—students at the University of Chicago in the classes of 1997 and 1998—to see if any remembered it, because "getting 2,424 respondents with refusals and callbacks would have required thousands and thousands of phone calls. Students would have had to spend many hours calling, which they and their friends would well remember." But Lott objected to this effort, Lindgren wrote, raising "serious questions about how complete the University's alumni records are." At that point Lindgren stopped, explaining that "my part in this affair is essentially done."[11]

Lott did provide one piece of direct evidence that he did the national survey—one person who said he had been telephoned as part of it. That person is David M. Gross, a Minnesota attorney who is also a former board member of the National Rifle Association and founding director of the Minnesota Gun Owners Civil Rights Association.[12] It seems extremely unlikely, to put it charitably, that he would turn up in a random sample of a few thousand people out of the 300 million Americans.

The conclusion seemed obvious: Lott had never done the national survey. He was lying.[13]

You might think that research fraud in the bible of gun rights owners would be a big story in the American media. But, in fact, it got almost no play. Lott did get fifteen minutes of fame in the mainstream media; however, that coverage focused not on his fraudulent statistics, but rather on the amusing story of his fictional web persona. The story was told beautifully by Richard Morin of the *Washington Post*:

> Mary Rosh thinks the world of John R. Lott Jr., the controversial American Enterprise Institute scholar whose book *More Guns, Less Crime* caused such a stir a few years ago.
>
> In postings on Web sites in this country and abroad, Rosh has tirelessly defended Lott against his harshest critics. He is a meticulous researcher, she's repeatedly told those who say otherwise. He's not driven by the ideology of the left or the

right. Rosh has even summoned memories of the classes she took from Lott a decade ago to illustrate Lott's probity and academic gifts.

"I have to say that he was the best professor I ever had," Rosh gushed in one Internet posting.

Indeed, Mary Rosh and John Lott agree about nearly everything.

Well they should, because Mary Rosh is John Lott.[14]

Lott quickly admitted he was guilty.

What's significant here is that the *Washington Post* coverage focused not on scandal around the fraudulent statistic that opens the influential book, but rather on the humorous story of the professor with the "cyber sock puppet." The report ran not as a news story about fraudulent gun research or a book story about a dishonest author, but rather in the *Post*'s "Style" section.

Even the *Chronicle of Higher Education* story on Lott was headlined "Scholar's most vigorous defender turns out to be himself, pseudonymously." The story surfaced in the *New York Times* in a cartoon in the *Book Review,* where Mark Alan Stamaty made fun of both Lott and Michael Bellesiles, starting with three panels where Bellesiles says (in Stamaty's words), "the data that backs up my thesis was destroyed in an office flood! HONEST!" This panel was followed by a slightly smaller one devoted to John Lott saying about his data "I had it in my computer, but my computer crashed and I lost it. HONEST!" Then came three more panels on Lott's "Mary Rosh" story.[15] That cartoon in the *Book Review* was the only coverage that Lott's research fraud received in the *New York Times*. (There were a few exceptions elsewhere in the media, which deserve credit: Timothy Noah writing in *Slate,* Ron Grossman in the *Chicago Tribune,* and especially Chris Mooney in *Mother Jones*).[16]

Lott defended himself in a letter published by the *Washington Post* in March 2003, where he said he was responding to an article that "questioned the existence of a 1997 survey that was used" in his book. Of course, he could have put it more directly, and without the passive voice: he could have written, "Critics questioned the existence of a 1997 survey I claim to have conducted." In his letter, he minimized the problem: "My discussion of the survey actually involved only one number in one sentence." Here "the survey" seems to exist. But "the bottom line is that I lost data for most of my various research projects, as well as the files for my book 'More Guns, Less Crime,' in a computer crash in July 1997."[17] There's a significant omission here: Lott does not say he lost the data for the 1997 survey he claims to have conducted—only that he lost the data for "most" of his research. And of course the critics by this time had been asking not only for the data, but the sample, the survey instrument, the names of the people who made the calls, the financial records of the project, the tally sheets, etc.—questions Lott knew well.

The letter continued, "With the help of other scholars . . . the massive data sets using county and state level crime data were reconstructed." However, that wasn't the data cited in the 1997 survey. The data whose existence was questioned by critics purported to describe a national telephone survey of gun brandishing, not crime data from counties and states.

"Academics have confirmed my hard-disk crash," he wrote in his letter to the *Washington Post*. But no one said he lied about a computer crash; they said he lied about having conducted a massive national telephone survey. The same unnamed "academics" are also described as having "confirmed . . . discussions that I had back in 1996 and 1997 regarding the survey." But when Duncan and Lambert examined these claims, they found that, while a couple of colleagues remembered discussing surveys in general with him, they did not recall discussing in 1997 a survey that Lott told them he himself was conducting. For example one of Lott's co-authors declared, "John told me that he had conducted a survey in 1997"—but significantly, that's not the same as "John told me in 1997 that he was conducting a survey."[18]

"There is also verification by a participant in the survey," Lott wrote. But this "participant" was that Minnesota attorney, the founding director of the Minnesota Gun Owners Civil Rights Association who claimed that, out of 300 million Americans, he received a random call from Lott's researchers.

Lott then declared in his letter to the *Post,* "I redid the survey last year and obtained similar results." However, doing a new survey does not establish that he told the truth when he wrote that he had conducted the "old" survey.

He wrote in the *Post,* "This data set and all the other data used in my new book, 'The Bias against Guns,' have also been made available to anyone who requests them at www.johnlott.org." At that website, he refers to "my two surveys" and repeats—twice—that "unfortunately the original 1997 sample was lost in a computer hard disk crash."[19] So the data is not available at the website, as promised in the *Post*. Thus, even in Lott's most recent work, he continues to make fraudulent claims about a survey he says he conducted.

On his website, he claims he never attributed the 98 percent figure to polls conducted by others—an attribution cited by his critics as evidence that he never conducted a survey himself. Here's what he wrote in several op-eds: "Polls by the *Los Angeles Times,* Gallup and Peter Hart Research Associates show that there are at least 760,000, and possibly as many as 3.6 million, defensive uses of guns per year. In 98 percent of the cases, such polls show, people simply brandish the weapon to stop an attack." At his website, he declares that the phrase "such polls" was "merely referring back to this type of polls and not those specific polls."[20] Of course, if there were other such polls, which showed what he claimed they did, then he should have named and cited those. You could call this discussion of the phrase "such polls" a misunderstanding of the English language, or you could call it a pathetic attempt at deception.

Lott continues to come up with arguments and defenses similar to this—when Chris Mooney interviewed him for *Mother Jones* for a September 2003 piece, Lott sent a blizzard of charts, tables, and e-mails with ever-shifting data sets and increasingly convoluted arguments.

Lott and his defenders argue that the 98 percent figure is not crucial to the argument in *More Guns, Less Crime*; it's true that the book contains many other more relevant statistics. Harvard economist David Hemenway explained what's wrong with that argument: one must have "faith in Lott's integrity" in order to accept the other statistical arguments he makes.[21]

What about the more relevant statistics supporting Lott's argument in *More Guns, Less Crime*? Lott had presented what he said was data on gun ownership and crime from all 3,054 U.S. counties from 1977 to 1992, which he said proved that the states with "concealed carry" laws had significantly lower rates of violent crime, especially rape and murder. Concealed handguns, Lott wrote, were "the most cost-effective method of reducing crime thus far analyzed by economists."[22] But two scholars writing in the *Journal of Legal Studies* conclude that small changes in Lott's data and statistical methodology produced drastically different results. In particular, if Florida was removed from the analysis, the evidence that concealed weapons reduced murder and rape disappeared completely.[23]

New research suggests Lott's thesis in *More Guns, Less Crime* is wrong: "concealed carry" laws do not reduce crime. The most important work on the topic appeared in the *Stanford Law Review,* which drew on more years of data and a slightly different methodology. The authors, Ian Ayres of the Yale Law School and John Donohue of Stanford Law School, concluded, "No longer can any plausible case be made on statistical grounds that shall-issue laws are likely to reduce crime for all or even most states." They found, on the contrary, that "concealed carry" laws might cause crime to increase.[24]

Unlike Bellesiles, Lott is not subject to academic sanction for research fraud because he does not currently hold an academic position. Indeed his academic career suggests that scholars don't consider his work to merit an academic position. He has held positions briefly at more than half a dozen universities, none of which decided to keep him. The pattern of his career is revealing: after earning a Ph.D. in economics at UCLA, he started out with a series of "visiting assistant professor" jobs at Texas A&M (1984–86), Rice, and UCLA's School of Management. Then he got a tenure track assistant professorship at the Wharton School at Penn, where he spent four years (1991–95) but failed to get tenure. He then went back to being a visiting assistant professor, this time at the University of Chicago business school (1994–95). At this point, it had been nine years since he started in his first academic job, which meant he should have qualified for a tenured position somewhere. But he didn't. Instead, he was rescued by the Olin Foundation, the right-wing organization that has funded dozens of conservative ideologues on college campuses,[25] and which gave him a four-year law and economics fellowship at the University of Chicago law school, where he wrote *More Guns, Less Crime.* That got him a position at Yale law school—not as a faculty member but as something called "senior research scholar." But things didn't pan out at Yale, and he ended up at the American Enterprise Institute in Washington D.C.[26]

The key fact for our purposes is that the mainstream media ignored what should have been a major story about research fraud in the bible of gun rights. A search of the Nexis database for "Lott" and "fraud" turns up a total of three articles that mention the fact that Lott has been accused of fraud: the *Chicago Tribune,* the *Chronicle of Higher Education,* and the *Washington Monthly.* (To that list should be added Timothy Noah in *Slate.*) Notably missing: the *New York Times,* the *Washington Post,* and the many newspapers that published

Lott's op-eds with the fraudulent claims: the *Wall Street Journal,* the *Los Angeles Times,* the *Chicago Sun-Times,* and the *Dallas Morning News,* among others.

In contrast, Nexis lists sixty-one news articles that link "Michael Bellesiles" and "fraud."[27]

The University of Chicago Press website continues to feature the Lott book prominently, with glorious blurbs from Milton Friedman, the *Wall Street Journal,* and *Business Week*; the press website contains no hint that the key statistic on page three of the book has been shown to be fraudulent.[28] In contrast, Vintage decided not to publish a second corrected edition of Bellesiles's book.

Lott is not a historian; he was trained as an economist. But because problems in his work have been compared so often with that of Bellesiles, it's appropriate to include his work here. Lott is defended by some of the same people who attacked Bellesiles, and he's been described by others as "the Bellesiles of the right."[29] Several writers have argued Lott and Bellesiles committed the same offense—research fraud. They make the same argument about Lott's missing study of gun brandishing and Bellesiles's flawed Table 1 about guns in probate records: since each author got one key piece of research wrong, how can we trust the rest of his work?

But the cases are different. There is no credible evidence that Lott ever did the national survey he claims to have done. In contrast, Bellesiles did research on the guns listed in probate records; where his figures were disputed, he returned to the archives in question, and in the second edition of his book, published a revised version of the flawed table; he also posted disputed probate documents on his website so that interested people can examine them.

Lott's website, in contrast, continues to make the claims shown to have been fraudulent.

What then explains the difference between the media treatment of Bellesiles and Lott? And what explains the fate of each? The charges in both cases were equally serious. The venues in which the debates took place were equally scholarly. The defense offered by Bellesiles was considerably more substantive and convincing than Lott's. The one great difference between the two cases is in the actions of the gun lobby. They mounted a massive campaign to destroy Bellesiles: to pressure Emory University to fire him, to demand that his publisher withdraw the book, and to insist that Columbia University withdraw the Bancroft Prize. But with Lott, the gun control lobby didn't mount any public campaign, didn't exert any pressure, didn't make any demands—didn't even demand that the newspapers that published Lott's fraudulent claims publish corrections. And no newspaper ever published a correction. Lott's critics were limited to scholars and journalists who restricted their efforts to the world of scholarly journals and a few news outlets like *Mother Jones* and *Slate*. Gun control advocates remained polite and reasonable, while the gun lobby shouted its demands.[30]

IV

Other Media Spectacles

IV

Other Media Spectacles

9

The "Porn Professor": Dino Cinel, Sexual Abuse, and the Catholic Church

A decade before the scandal over clerical sex abuse rocked the Catholic Church, a single case surfaced in academia, in the history department of the City University of New York's College of Staten Island.[1] Here a historian got into trouble for having had sex with young people, and the case made page one of the local papers and became the lead item on TV news in New York City. This offense, far from an academic one—far from plagiarism or unreliable research, easily understood by the public—was one that you might think would unite the community and the profession in a clear statement that a record of such offenses disqualified one from teaching. Yet the professor found defenders who had the power and the skill to delay the disciplinary process for five years. The case of the "porn professor" raises the questions, what are the grounds for firing a tenured faculty member? And who has the power to challenge university decisions in such matters?

The story begins in 1990, when New York City's Italian-American leaders had been unhappy with the City University for a long time. Several CUNY professors that year formed the Italian-American Legal Defense and Higher Education Fund, which filed a class-action suit with the U.S. Department of Labor, claiming that the university discriminated against Italian-Americans in its hiring of faculty. In response, the state legislature, under pressure from Italian-American representatives, established a new position at the City University: Distinguished Professor of Italian-American Immigration History. The professorship was assigned to CUNY's College of Staten Island, located in the borough with the largest proportion of Italian-Americans. A nationwide search was conducted, and the prestigious new post was awarded to a professor from Tulane University, Dino Cinel. When he arrived at Staten Island in February 1991, the local Italian-American politicians and community leaders scrambled to have their pictures taken with him.[2]

But three months after he began teaching—at a salary of $90,000, the top of the scale in 1990—the media reported that Cinel was a former priest who had been defrocked two years earlier; and that he had been defrocked after the Church discovered 160 hours of homemade pornographic videotapes showing him engaging in oral sex, anal sex, and group sex with at least seven different teenage boys. Cinel's pornographic photos of one of the young men had been published in the Danish magazine *Dreamboy USA*. They also found an extensive collection of commercially produced kiddie porn in his room at the rectory, including films of children performing oral sex on adult men.[3]

The discovery of these materials had been kept secret for two years, first by the Church, and then by the district attorney in New Orleans. After the story broke, the D.A. filed criminal charges against Cinel; two of the young men in the videos had already filed civil suits against him, and they were interviewed on TV, describing how they had been exploited and deceived by "Father Dino." Geraldo Rivera showed some of the homemade videos on his TV show *Now It Can Be Told,* including one showing Cinel in bed with two teenage boys.[4]

The Italian-American community on Staten Island was outraged, and the university administration agreed that Cinel's record made him unfit for the job. But he had been hired with tenure. To fire a tenured professor in the City University is an extremely time-consuming procedure, governed by a collective bargaining agreement with the American Federation of Teachers. As a faculty member, Cinel was entitled to union representation. So the A.F.T. affiliate that represents CUNY faculty—the Professional Staff Congress—went to bat for Cinel, defending him against the university's attempt to fire him. The charge was "conduct unbecoming a member of the staff," and the A.F.T. argued that he was not guilty and should not be fired.[5]

His defense was surprisingly strong: He said he checked the ages of his sex partners in New Orleans, and determined that they were all above the state's legal age of consent—seventeen. The D.A. in New Orleans had filed a single charge against him—possession of child pornography—but the case hadn't come to trial when CUNY was trying to fire him. He had never been indicted for, much less convicted of, having sex with a minor. He pointed out that he had never been convicted of any criminal sex offense. The two civil suits filed by young men in the videos had not come to trial. There was no evidence he ever made sexual advances to students in his eleven years at Tulane or to any of his parishioners at St. Rita's Church; he said he met all his partners in the French Quarter.[6]

Since the people he had sex with were consenting adults, Cinel and his defenders argued, his personal life was none of the university's business—and certainly not grounds for firing him. The university, in this view, was caving in to homophobic hysteria. His defenders recalled that, during the McCarthy era, universities bowed to another wave of hysteria and fired professors for things unrelated to their job performance or qualifications. Cinel also said he received therapy for what he called an "addiction," and that he had become a different man, married with a two-year-old daughter. The union fought hard for the principle that employees should be fired only for unacceptable performance on the job.[7]

Did Cinel abuse his position of authority as a priest to sexually exploit teenage boys? Or was he a victim who had his private sexual preferences made public in a homophobic society? Did Cinel commit fraud in concealing his troubled past from the college search committee? Or was he under no obligation to reveal accusations about his private life that he considered untrue and irrelevant to his job qualifications? Should students at the College of Staten Island be protected from him, or should the university stand up and protect a professor from a new sexual McCarthyism? And who had the power to decide? The Dino Cinel case stood at the intersection of civil libertarian concerns about privacy rights, gay concerns about homophobia, labor concerns about job security, and parental concerns about the sexual abuse of young people.

Although Cinel was "not available for an interview," according to his union attorney, Nick Russo, interviews with his colleagues, union and Academic Senate officials, and others familiar with the case made it possible to outline his defense.[8] At the top of the list was the absence of a criminal conviction. Cinel's defenders argued that professors should be stripped of tenure only for the most serious offenses, proven in a court of law. Even then, only some criminal convictions were relevant, depending on the crime—civil disobedience in a political protest would not be grounds for firing a professor, while the tax fraud conviction of a professor of tax law provided grounds for disciplinary action by the University of Minnesota. At the University of California, regulations state that professors can be fired for misconduct outside the university only after the "commission of a criminal act . . . has led to conviction in a court of law and which clearly demonstrates unfitness to continue as a member of the faculty."[9] But Cinel had not been convicted of anything.

If Cinel had never been convicted, he had been charged—with possession of child pornography—and probably would have been convicted a couple of years before the issue surfaced in New York—if there had not been a cover-up instigated by the Church and joined by the New Orleans district attorney. The New Orleans D.A. at that time, and for the previous fifteen years, was Harry Connick Sr., father of the pop singer. Although the D.A. testified before the state legislature in favor of one of the country's fiercest antiporn laws, he was also a parishioner at St. Rita's, where Cinel celebrated mass and heard confessions. Cinel had been a guest in Connick's home, and had presided at his brother-in-law's wedding. When the archdiocese handed over Cinel's videos to the D.A., they were accompanied by a letter that concluded, "This action on the part of the Archdiocese should therefore not be considered by your office in any way seeking the initiation of criminal charges with respect to this material or any activities of Dr. Cinel in relation thereto." Connick obligingly kept the entire case secret for two years, explaining later that he didn't want to embarrass "Holy Mother the Church." The cover-up was eventually shattered by a local TV investigative reporter, Richard Angelico.[10]

Cinel also could have been prosecuted by federal authorities for manufacture and transportation of child pornography—although he was not. Officials of the Postal Service and U.S. Customs met in July 1989 with Chris Fontaine, one of the young men in the videos, and showed him a copy of *Dreamboy USA* magazine. The entire issue consisted of pornographic pictures of Fontaine—pictures taken by Cinel and mailed to the magazine—in which Fontaine is shown pulling down his briefs, displaying his erections, and masturbating. When Fontaine saw the pictures, according to one authority on the case, "he began crying." The feds decided not to charge Cinel, but rather to leave the prosecution to the New Orleans D.A., apparently because it would be easier to win a conviction under Louisiana law. (Fontaine filed a civil suit charging Cinel with violation of privacy in the publication of the photos, which had not been heard at the time of the City University proceedings.)[11]

The D.A. also could have charged Cinel with statutory rape, but he accepted Cinel's argument that all the young people in the videos were over seventeen. He could have charged Cinel with producing pornography, which is a crime in Louisiana. (Cinel also could have been prosecuted for the acts in the videos; at the time, sodomy was a "crime against nature" in Louisiana—although a sodomy prosecution would not have provided a legitimate basis for firing him from the City University.) But the Catholic D.A. went easy on the priest, charging him only with a single count of possession of child pornography, which had not come to trial at the time of the scandals on Staten Island, because Cinel had filed an appeal with the state supreme court, seeking to throw out the indictment on the grounds that he had been told he wouldn't be prosecuted. Ray Bigelow, first assistant D.A. in New Orleans, told me at the time, "We intend to try Mr. Cinel," but reporter Angelico, who broke the story, said, "That'll be the day. In my interview with Harry Connick at the time, he told me he was not going to prosecute any priest over a bunch of dirty pictures. I'm convinced Cinel will get a free ride."[12]

But the fact that Cinel had not been convicted of a criminal offense did not mean he couldn't be fired. The prevailing standard for firing someone from an academic job, according to Ernst Benjamin, then executive director of the American Association of University Professors, is only "reasonableness." The officials who would decide Cinel's fate as a CUNY professor were to be reasonable in deciding what evidence of wrongdoing they would consider and how much weight to give it. It was reasonable for the City University to consider Cinel's conduct in his job as a priest, even if there had been no criminal conviction.[13]

Cinel's defenders argued also that the conduct which the university regarded as "unbecoming" concerned his private life, not his job performance. He had a privacy right under the Constitution, which the university as a public institution was required to recognize; since he had not been charged with wrongdoing in the conduct of his job, his defenders argued, there were no legitimate grounds for firing him. "We're no longer living according to the standards of *The Donna Reed Show,*" Richard Gid Powers, a colleague of Cinel's in the history department at the College of Staten Island, told me at the time. "Standards of personal life have changed—the public doesn't have the right to get into Cinel's private life."[14]

The only reason we know about Cinel's private life at all, in this view, is that his privacy rights were violated by the New Orleans television station that reported on claims made in the civil suit filed by one of the boys. But, Cinel's defenders argued, civil suits about private sexual conduct should not be considered relevant to hiring and firing. Cinel's argument was that he was careful to compartmentalize his life, separating work and sex. He liked having sex with young men, and he found willing adult partners on the streets of the French Quarter. That, he argued, was nobody's business but his own.[15]

Although Cinel was never accused of sexual misconduct in his work at Tulane, he *was* fired from his job as a priest because of sexual misconduct in his work. And the facts which led the Church to fire him made his sex life relevant to his qualifications as a professor: he abused his authority (as a priest) to sexually exploit young people. And his job as a professor gave him authority over young people.

The evidence here was strong: when Chris Fontaine got in trouble with the police, Cinel went to court and persuaded the judge to release Fontaine on probation under the priest's supervision. "Father is willing to work with you to help you," the judge told Fontaine. "I hope that will be sufficient to get you on the right track, young man." Fontaine reported that after that, whenever he resisted Cinel's sexual demands, Cinel would threaten to have him sent to prison. Cinel's criminal lawyer denied Fontaine's account. Another of Cinel's partners, Ronnie Tichenor, who said he was thirteen when Cinel began having sex with him, said the priest "told me he was looking out for my welfare, that he could help me better achieve an education and a better position in life." At the time, Tichenor was living in New Orleans at a home for runaway youth.[16]

Cinel abused his authority as a priest to gain sex partners in other ways—by inviting them to have sex in the rectory; and, according to one of the young men suing him, by invoking his knowledge of "God's will." One of the young people told reporter Angelico that Cinel told him "it was God's will that we had love for one another and that sex was the best way for us to show it." According to Fontaine, he first met Cinel one afternoon in New Orleans's Jackson Square, the tourist center of town; "He came walking up to me . . . and he started telling me he was a priest," Fontaine told Angelico. "We became friends." On their second or third meeting, Cinel "asked me if I smoked weed"; they smoked marijuana together, Fontaine said, and then Father Dino "started rubbing his hands on me and told me he wanted to give me a massage. . . . Then he told me to take off my clothes. He just told me to leave my underwear on, and it went from there. He started masturbating me, and I tried to get away; he held me down for a minute and told me, 'Just relax and close your eyes.' He put it in my head that they did it in Greek days and it's all right."[17]

But Fontaine was not a credible source, Cinel's defenders argued. Cinel said Fontaine was a gay hustler working the French Quarter after dark. Indeed, Cinel asserted that since he was a priest and Fontaine was a street hustler, "I was the best person he could have sex with." Fontaine had "a passion to get to the church's deep pockets," according to the union's lawyer, Nick Russo, and was making harmful statements about Cinel in the hopes of winning his lawsuit, which would force the church to pay him damages.[18]

The City University search committee that recommended Cinel for the distinguished professor position had not known that he was a defrocked priest, because he never told them. The *curriculum vitae* that Cinel submitted along with his job application described only his academic qualifications. Cinel listed no B.A. degree, only an M.A. and Ph.D. He had no B.A. because he had attended seminary instead of college. The search committee understood that before getting his M.A. from NYU, he had been a student in his native Italy; they did not inquire further.[19]

Was Cinel under an obligation to disclose potentially damaging information to the City University search committee? "Only if it was relevant to his employment," said Matt Finkin, distinguished professor of law at the University of Illinois, Urbana-Champaign, and a specialist in personnel, employment, and arbitration.[20] Search committees have a reasonable expectation that applications will be complete and truthful. The relevant information in this case was that Cinel had been dismissed from a previous job—serving as a priest—because of abuse of authority: sexual misconduct involving young people. If Cinel's résumé had included the information that he had been a priest, the search committee would have asked why he left the priesthood, and thus probably would have learned the whole story. Indeed, the charges of abuse of power—sexual misconduct involving young people—would be relevant to his job qualifications even if he had not lost a job because of it.

His conduct in New Orleans should not automatically have disqualified him from the job, but it certainly was a relevant consideration for the search committee. Cinel should have summarized for the committee the charges and his defense, explaining why the College of Staten Island could be confident that, if they hired him, he would not engage in any sexual misconduct on the job.

He didn't do that because he knew he wouldn't have gotten the post. The advertisements for the position listed special administrative duties associated with this "distinguished" professorship, including community outreach and liaison with the Italian-American community of Staten Island. Whoever got the job was supposed to help recruit and retain Italian-American students, to work with them to overcome their high dropout rate and their status within the City University as an "under-represented group." The university administration's view was that his conduct in New Orleans made him unfit for that position, and that, by concealing the information that he had been a priest, he secured the job by fraud. And contracts entered into fraudulently are not binding.[21]

Cinel's defenders argued that the New Orleans events made him unfit for the job only because of the homophobia on Staten Island, and for the City University to bow to that would amount to discrimination. Besides, Cinel had been led to believe he had an agreement with the church and the New Orleans D.A. that would keep his misconduct confidential, and thus the citizens of Staten Island would never learn about his sex life. Therefore, in this view, he did not intentionally commit fraud.

The university had an obligation not to endorse the homophobic views held by many people on Staten Island. But it also had an obligation to protect its students. What made Cinel unfit was not a homosexual past but rather sexual abuse of power in relation to young people. If a forty-five-year-old man had used his influence as a priest to have sex with a thirteen-year-old girl, that former priest should also have been found unsuitable.

Cinel's defenders argued that teenage boys who have sex with older men are not exclusively victims; in many cases, they are capable of making a choice; some are willing and indeed eager partners. Cinel said that, on his arrival as a priest in New Orleans, he called the District Attorney's office to ask what the legal age of consent was in Louisiana, and learned it was seventeen. Henceforth, he says, he was careful to ask his potential sex partners whether they were seventeen, and to have sex with them only if they said they were.

"But why believe Dino?" one of his critics asked. "If he didn't say that, he'd be admitting he was guilty of statutory rape." In his deposition describing checking one partner's ID, he admitted that he didn't see a name or a picture on the ID card, just a birth date.[22] And in May 1991, according to the *Staten Island Advance,* Cinel admitted that his homemade videos "featured three or four boys who might have been under 17 and minors. 'They could have been under-age,' he said. 'They didn't carry identification papers with them.' "[23] Cinel's claim that he made sure his teenage sex partners were of the age of consent wasn't convincing.

Of the two boys in the tapes who had been identified, Fontaine said he was seventeen at the time, but Tichenor said he was only thirteen when the priest began having sex with him. In the videos that were shown on TV, Cinel's partners *look* young. Reporter Richard Angelico noted that Church officials had Cinel's home-made videotapes for three months before turning them over to the D.A.; he suspected that the Church removed tapes involving very young teenagers, like the thirteen-year-old, during that period. Church officials insisted they gave the D.A. all the tapes.[24]

But even if every one of Cinel's sex partners was seventeen or older, it was still an abuse of power for a priest to use his authority to have sex with them. The issue was not their conduct, but rather his. The statements made by the two young men in their civil suits suggested how Cinel drew on their youth and his authority as a priest to manipulate them into becoming his sex partners. Leslie Bennetts investigated the case for *Vanity Fair;* she reported that both Chris Fontaine and Ronnie Tichenor came from troubled families, which lacked a stable father figure; Fontaine was, according to Bennetts, "borderline retarded." Fontaine told Angelico in a TV interview, "My parents didn't care about me, and I didn't have nothing. . . . He made me believe that I was a kid in need of a fa-ther and he was a father in need of a son, and God put us together to help each other and to serve each other's needs."[25] This doesn't sound like the relationship between consenting adults that Cinel claimed it was. People say many things to persuade others to have sex with them, but when a priest in the church rectory invokes God's will, he crosses the line into abuse of authority.

It was certainly relevant to his job performance that this man sought out sex partners who were the age of the students at the College of Staten Island. His abuse of power in relation to young people—even though they were not his students—was relevant to his qualifications as a college teacher.

Irwin H. Polishook was president of the Professional Staff Congress of the American Federation of Teachers affiliate that defended Cinel against the university's attempt to fire him. When I asked how the union defined the issues in the case, he replied, "We're trying to protect somebody who's a professor. We believe they can't dismiss him for the cause they've outlined in their complaint." What was wrong in the university's complaint? "I won't tell you what their complaint is," he replied, explaining, "If somebody accused you of something you knew wasn't true, you wouldn't want it out." But wasn't it true that Cinel was defrocked after the discovery of 160 hours of videos of himself having sex with young men in the rectory, and after his photos of one of them were published in *Dreamboy USA*? "Our job is to protect him, and we will protect him." Did the union think he should be permitted to return to classroom teaching? "We will defend his right to remain a professor."[26]

"Dino has manipulated the system," said Jason Berry, a Catholic journalist who wrote about the Cinel case. "It's a disgrace. If the union can't muster any outrage over what he's done, then shame on them."[27] Cinel's sex life was indeed relevant to his job as a teacher, argued New Orleans private investigator Gary Raymond, a consultant for the plaintiffs' attorneys in the two civil suits. Raymond was one of the few people to have seen all 160 hours of Cinel's homemade videos. "This guy gets me," he said in an interview. "He's picking on the weakest, most vulnerable members of society. He does it without remorse. He is a horrible individual. This guy teaching? Oh, man. He shouldn't be anywhere he has any kind of control of any young person. A kid in college included. There's no way he should be there. Ever."[28]

Still others argued that although what Cinel had done was reprehensible, he shouldn't be fired for it. Sandi Cooper was vice chair of the executive committee of the university-wide faculty senate of CUNY and professor of history at the College of Staten Island and the Graduate Center. "Sexual abuse of power is absolutely misconduct," she told me. "What he did is horrifying. He should be indicted and prosecuted. But I also believe that it's dangerous to break tenure in this university in this political climate. I remember McCarthyism. If the guy had done something in our classrooms, there wouldn't be any question. But we're dealing here with unproven charges. He can't be returned to the classroom, but the university could bury him in some administrative job where he could use his research skills. On the other hand, if he were convicted, that would change the story."[29]

Would it be McCarthyism to fire Cinel? When professors and others were fired in the fifties, it was because of their political beliefs and affiliations, not their actions. It would be McCarthyism if the City University tried to fire Cinel for having belonged to the

North American Man-Boy Love Association. But the case against Cinel did not concern his beliefs or affiliations; it concerned his actions, actions relevant to his job.

At the very least, Cinel should have been fired for deception—for fraud in the hiring process. By concealing the information that he had been fired from a previous job for charges of sexual abuse of power involving young people, Cinel deceived the university about his qualifications to serve as the distinguished professor of Italian-American history. His job history was especially relevant in view of the fact that the new job involved recruiting and retaining young Italian-Americans at the college. He concealed information he rightly feared would disqualify him.

It took a long time for the university to fire him. The process began in the summer of 1991; two years later, the university's administrative hearing officer ruled that Cinel should be fired. The union appealed that decision, which then went to arbitration. If the arbitrator's decision had gone against Cinel, he then had the right to go to court to have it overturned. At this point, the taxpayers of New York City were paying Cinel an annual salary of close to $70,000, and he was not teaching.[30]

In 1993, Cinel was stripped of his title as "Distinguished Professor," but because he had tenure, he remained on the payroll at CUNY, assigned to "non-classroom duties," which Ron Grossman of the *Chicago Tribune* described as "essentially make-work," while the union appealed his case.[31] That took another two years; Cinel was finally dismissed from his position as professor at the City University on February 14, 1995.[32]

"The issue here is not life-style choice or privacy, but sexual abuse, the abuse of power, and fraud," said David Nasaw, a historian at the City University who served on the search committee that hired Cinel. "The whole thing is a travesty."[33]

Then in 2003, History News Network published an article showing that Cinel's research in his 1982 book, *From Italy to San Francisco,* was fraudulent. The documents he cited on Italian immigration to the U.S. didn't exist, and his footnotes were described by Sebastian Fichera as "a relentless program of obfuscation."[34]

Meanwhile, the lawsuit that had led to Cinel's hiring in the first place—in which the Italian-American Legal Defense and Higher Education Fund argued that the City University discriminated against Italian-American faculty members—was settled by the university. Under the terms of the settlement, the university's Italian-American Institute became a unit of Queens College. In addition, the college agreed to appoint a distinguished professor of Italian-American studies.[35]

10

Lying to Students About Vietnam: The Mythic Past of Joseph Ellis

*P*rofessor's Past in Doubt": that was the headline on page one of
the *Boston Globe* in June 2001, and that story created a classic
media spectacle around Joseph Ellis, who, as the paper reported, had
become "a national literary icon" for his 1997 Jefferson biography.
He had recently won the Pulitzer Prize for History for *Founding
Brothers: The Revolutionary Generation,* which was on the bestseller
list as the scandal broke. The paper described him as "a beloved
mentor to many students" at Mount Holyoke, an elite women's college in New England, where he had taught for twenty-nine years,
"perhaps the college's most popular and engaging professor."[1]

The personal past that was "in doubt" concerned Ellis's statements to students in lectures that he had fought in Vietnam and
then joined the antiwar movement. He had said, the *Globe* reported,

that he "went to Vietnam in 1965 as a platoon leader and para-trooper with the 101st Airborne Division."[2] That was the year President Johnson first sent regular army units, including the 101st, into the war zone.

He also said, according to the *Globe,* that in Vietnam he had worked in Saigon on the staff of General William C. Westmoreland, commander of American forces; and that he had shared his views of Westmoreland with David Halberstam, who was writing what would become the 1972 bestseller *The Best and the Brightest.*

The *Globe* reported that Ellis also said that, after finishing his tour of duty in Vietnam, he "joined the peace movement while at Yale—motivated to do so by what he had seen in Vietnam."[3]

And then the *Globe* reported that none of this was true. Ellis had been an undergrad at William and Mary, where he joined ROTC and earned a second lieutenant commission when he graduated in 1965. He deferred his active duty in order to attend graduate school in history at Yale. After received his Ph.D. in 1969, he spent two months in an officer's basic course at Fort Gordon, Georgia, and then in October 1969 joined the faculty at West Point and began teaching history there—which he did until 1972, when he was discharged as a captain. The *Globe* quoted a former colleague of his in the West Point history department who had previously served as an infantry company commander in Vietnam; he said that Ellis once told him, "Why should I go be a ground-pounder in Vietnam when I can polish my academic credentials here at West Point?"[4]

The *Globe* story went on to demolish Ellis's claims that he had been active in the antiwar and civil rights movements. First, they quoted a student who recalled what Ellis had said in class: "He was the veteran who came back and participated in the antiwar movement. So his perspective is very liberal." But "the *Globe* could find no evidence that he was in any visible way part of the antiwar movement." His thesis adviser at Yale, Edmond Morgan, "expressed surprise at the notion" that Ellis had been an antiwar activist. And Gaddis Smith, another Yale historian who had supervised the graduate program in Ellis's day and had written about the antiwar movement at Yale, told the *Globe,* "Joe was a superb student. But an antiwar activist? I don't recall anything like that."[5]

On civil rights, the *Globe* quoted Ellis as having said he "spent a summer doing civil rights work in Mississippi." In lectures he had described incidents where local police "pounded on his door at night" and another time when state police followed his car. But according to the *Globe,* all he had ever done was "visit the South to enlist students" for the "Yale Intensive Studies Program for Minority Students" in 1969, several years after the heyday of student civil rights activism in the South.[6]

The most devastating part of the *Globe* story came next: comments from seven Mount Holyoke and Amherst students who had taken Ellis's courses and then learned of his lies. They all said that Ellis's accounts of his experiences in Vietnam were memorable and stimulated class discussions. One who took Ellis's course "The Literature on Vietnam" said, "The course was something so central to him because he did serve there." When teaching, the student said, "He uses different anecdotes from his own personal experience in Vietnam . . . to help us understand it better. But he doesn't want to force feed the class his personal views. He does have a very objective view of the war. He is able to step back from his own war experience in Vietnam."[7]

Another said Ellis's personal stories about fighting in Vietnam "changed the dimension of the course." "His having that personal experience gave the course more gravity. He was honest about his experience in the war and its effect on him as a person," the student said. "The course allowed me to imagine myself in the circumstances he faced. Having the course taught by someone who was there helped." That student described a moving moment in one class, when Ellis "told us about a fellow, a strong jock, a college football player, who was drafted and came to Vietnam. They were out in the field, and this guy was reading Emily Dickinson poems that brought him to tears. That was the kind of stress these men were placed under."[8]

"The course was very meaningful for me," he concluded. "I'm staring down the barrel of graduation, and I think back to that course and how the war was a test of his manhood. . . . It almost made me a tad jealous of people who had that choice to make— whether to go or not. He had gone, taken the test of manhood, and passed it." Told that Ellis had been lying about his service in Vietnam, that student told the *Globe* he was "offended and shocked."[9]

A second student—an Amherst senior who took the same class—also recalled Ellis talking about how he had "served honorably in Vietnam out of a sense of duty." That student also said he was "shocked and perplexed" at the deception.[10]

The *Globe* ran the story at the top of page one. Clearly, they thought a history professor inventing a history for himself was big

news. The questions quickly became, how bad is it to lie to students in class? And what is the appropriate penalty?

The answers to those questions ranged across the full spectrum. On
one end, some suggested Ellis should be fired if he didn't resign. At
the other, the *Globe* was attacked for "gotcha journalism" in going
after Ellis.

The second response came from the president of Mount Holyoke,
Joanne V. Creighton, who rushed to Ellis's defense, dismissed the
relevance of his lying to students, and attacked the *Globe* for publishing the story. She defended what she called Ellis's "great integrity, honesty, and honor," and said, "We at the college do not
know what public interest the *Globe* is trying to serve through a
story of this nature."

Creighton was immediately hit with the kind of firestorm of
criticism that occurs only in the middle of a media spectacle. The
Lexis-Nexis database lists dozens of newspapers and magazines
that repeated and criticized Creighton's defense—making it by far
the most quoted statement she ever made in her career. She is also
an English professor who had written books on Joyce Carol Oates
and Margaret Drabble, but her statement attacking the *Globe*
got about eighty times more attention than anything she ever
wrote about fiction. The *New Republic* comment was typical. Its
editors took up her questioning what interest the *Globe* was serving by publishing their story. "The interest," the *New Republic* editors wrote, "is historical truth—a commodity whose importance
Ellis, as one of the nation's most visible historians, is supposed to

cherish. And which the administration of Mount Holyoke evidently does not."[11]

Much of the press response was even more brutal. The *New York Post,* in an editorial, called Ellis "a weasel," and then declared, "Here's a bigger weasel: Mt. Holyoke College President Joanne V. Creighton." The paper continued, "She's either a liar herself, which is quite possible, or a moron."[12]

The case against Ellis was made in an op-ed in the *Globe* by David J. Garrow, like Ellis a Pulitzer Prize winner and a biographer of great men (in his case, Martin Luther King Jr.), as well as presidential distinguished professor at Emory University School of Law.[13] He argued that Ellis should be barred from "ever again taking the podium in a college classroom," adding that, "if Ellis does not have the personal good judgment to remove himself from teaching, then the administration and trustees of Mount Holyoke owe it to their students to protect the honesty and integrity of the classroom" by firing him. Garrow insisted that "knowingly false teaching is a professional and ethical offense of the highest order." He blasted Mount Holyoke president Creighton's criticism of the *Globe* as "an even greater academic disgrace than Ellis's fictions." Creighton, he wrote, was saying "they have a dramatically lower standard for truth-in-teaching at Mount Holyoke College than what is imposed upon professors' published writings." Garrow insisted that "one's obligation to be honest and truthful in the classroom is in no way less constant and demanding than one's obligation to be honest and truthful with every sentence or footnote one puts into print." Ellis should not only be fired from Mount Holyoke, he concluded, but "barred from ever again teaching history" anywhere.[14]

Garrow's argument was widely quoted and cited in publications including *Time* magazine and *Newsday;* the *Los Angeles Times* quoted him in an editorial arguing that "a scholar's right to privacy does not include the right to deceive his students and the public," and concluding that "Ellis should go." The *Chicago Tribune* also cited Garrow in asking how any college "could justify retaining a faculty member guilty of such grievous violations of the truth."[15]

Most of Ellis's defenders did not take up Garrow's argument; instead, they focused on Ellis's own suffering as a significant punishment. The *Washington Post* story quoted an unnamed "longtime friend" who said Ellis "was in tremendous pain." Donal O'Shea, dean of faculty at Mount Holyoke, told the *Post,* "He cares so deeply about students. I find it hard to believe he was deliberately misleading them."[16] Others minimized the seriousness of the offense: Ashbel Green, Ellis's editor at Knopf, told the *Los Angeles Times,* "I don't know anybody who hasn't exaggerated his past in some fashion, not perhaps as much as he did. It seems to be part of human nature." Recalling an old adage, Green said: "The older a man gets, the faster he ran as a boy."[17]

Only one publication joined Creighton in criticizing the *Globe* for publishing the story—the *Atlantic* magazine website. There, Jack Beatty argued that Ellis was not a "public figure" and thus should not have been the subject of "a front-page mugging." He explicitly challenged the argument that lying to students was just as bad as lying to readers: "If the *Globe* had found that Ellis had falsified material in his Pulitzer Prize–winning book, that would have provided a public peg to look into his on-the-job tale-telling. But, on the contrary, the historians quoted by the *Globe* unanimously said that his scholarly work was beyond reproach." Yes, Ellis had "led his students to believe" he had fought in Vietnam. But that, Beatty argued, had "no malign consequences." The only "malign consequences," he argued, were those suffered by Ellis as a result of the *Globe*'s exposé.[18]

He concluded, "Who among us has not done the same or worse? Joseph Ellis . . . deceived people about his own life, something every adult does to varying degrees." Beatty thought the classroom lies might have made for good teaching: "Ellis is known for the you-are-there quality of his historical writing. Maybe this was you-are-there teaching." Finally, Ellis had a "privacy right" to "fabulate."[19]

Beatty gave some answers to Creighton's question about the *Globe*'s possible motives in publishing its story: "Profit comes first with them. Business imperatives drive stories like the one on Ellis. . . . As the drive for profit sanctions more and more lurid snooping on ordinary citizens, we need protection against the media." Finally came the argument he considered the clincher: "Norman Mailer, a Pulitzer winner, has spent a career boasting of his prowess as a lover. Will the *Globe* now interview his lovers to test his veracity about his virility?"[20]

Then Beatty reversed course and conceded that lying to students in class was not a good thing. But what should the *Globe* have done about that? Beatty concluded that the *Globe* should not have printed the story. Instead, it should have acted privately to deter Ellis from lying to students in the future: "The *Globe* should have put Ellis on notice: we know you were not in Vietnam, and if you tell future students or interviewers that you were, and we find out, we will publish our story. If Ellis then stopped lying, the *Globe* would have achieved the same end, but without ruining Ellis's reputation."[21]

Only one writer bothered to take up Beatty's arguments: Geneva Overholser in the *Seattle Post-Intelligencer*. Her argument was simple and hard to refute: "The role of the media is not to blackmail, but to publish. If information is sound and significant, the media should put it out."[22]

There were many other problems with Beatty's piece: lying to students in class is worse than lying to acquaintances because students are a captive audience in a setting committed to truth seeking. Teachers do not have a "privacy right" to lie to students in class. Lies do not make for good teaching.

Two months after the *Globe* published its story, Mount Holyoke announced the punishment for Ellis: as recommended by "a college committee," he would be suspended for a year without pay, stripped of his endowed chair as Ford Foundation Professor of History, and barred from teaching his course on Vietnam. President Creighton said, "I strongly rebuke Professor Ellis for his lie about his military experience. Perpetuated over many years, his lie about himself clearly violates the ethics of our profession and the integrity we expect of all members of our community. . . . It was a particularly egregious failing in a teacher of history. Misleading students is wrong and nothing can excuse it."[23]

Ellis did not comment, but in a statement released by Mount Holyoke, he said he accepted the punishment: "By misrepresenting my military service to students in the course on the Vietnam War, I did something both stupid and wrong," he said. "I apologize to the students, as well as to the faculty of this institution, for violating the implicit covenant of trust that must exist in the classroom. Finally, I apologize to those Vietnam veterans who have expressed their understandable anger about my lie. I am truly sorry for the hurt I have caused."[24]

The punishment was one of the most severe ever given to a tenured professor, and, given the offense, seems appropriate: a year without pay, the loss of an endowed chair, and a ban on teaching about Vietnam. The loss of the endowed chair meant a significant loss in research funds.

The punishment was met in many quarters with skepticism. The *Boston Globe* pointed out that other senior professors caught lying had been forced to resign, and cited three recent cases.[25] The *Hartford Courant* editorial was representative: "It isn't as if he's been permanently exiled," the editors wrote, and went on to quote from President Creighton's letter to the college community: "The advisory committee and I believe that Mount Holyoke College can unequivocally condemn Professor Ellis' lie and impose significant sanctions, at the same time that it can accept his apology and make room for his return and future service to the college." The *Courant* commented: "So, a welcome back in the same breath as the condemnation. That takes the sting out of it."[26]

They might also have pointed out that Creighton minimized Ellis's offenses by referring to "lie" in the singular. The only "lie" she "rebuked" him for was claiming to have served in Vietnam. Apparently it was not wrong to lie about having been an activist in the antiwar and civil rights movements.

*   *   *

Some high-profile mainstream publications had no trouble publishing Ellis soon after the revelations of his lying. The *New Yorker* didn't explain when, four months after the *Globe* story, it published a big (4,500 word) Ellis piece about Alexander Hamilton.[27] Other publications, however, felt it necessary to make the case for bringing him back as a contributor.

The *New York Times* took the lead in making the case for Ellis. The paper argued, both in the *Book Review* and on the editorial page, that lying to students in class was not so bad, and therefore Ellis should be forgiven. Just a few weeks after the story broke in the *Globe,* the *Times Book Review* ran a commentary by Judith Shulevitz on its prestigious back page. The first two paragraphs praised Ellis to the skies for his magnificent books on Adams and Jefferson. She invoked Edmund Wilson and added some thoughts about the good qualities "Ellis shares with Sophocles." Then came the crucial argument: "Ellis's strengths as a writer bear keeping in mind as we consider his weakness as a man." The former were more significant than the latter. And "in his work, if not in his life, Ellis has never crossed the line between fiction and history."[28]

Shulevitz compared Ellis to the subjects of his prizewinning books, Adams and Jefferson—books where he revealed the tragic flaws of great men. Her conclusion compared Ellis to Sophocles once again: he was "a prodigiously gifted storyteller" with an "easy way of slipping inside other people's heads," which "first serves him well, then runs away with him and gets him into trouble." She meant that his storytelling ability led him to lie to students about his own life.

Ellis had suffered, Shulevitz argued, and his readers benefited from that suffering: "Surely Ellis has struggled before with his own darker impulses. . . . As [Edmund] Wilson says of Sophocles, . . . he couldn't have written the way he did without intimate knowledge of inner torment." This imagined torment over his lying to students enabled him to write the great books he gave us.

Thus, she concluded, "by dint of talent, celebrity and the gotcha tactics of modern journalism, he has become one of his own, a hero with a tragic flaw. Happily, however, when emotions subside, we'll realize that he falls well short of being Sophoclean. So he lied! A foolish thing to do, but his work holds up anyway."[29] The end.

The line "so he lied!" misses the key fact: Ellis lied to students, in the classroom—to a captive audience in a setting committed to the search for truth; Ellis lied to students required to attend and take notes on his lectures, students who would be tested and graded by him.

Shulevitz's defense of Ellis boiled down to two arguments: first, lying to students must have caused him "inner torment," which enabled him to write great biographies of great men—although the biographies had already been written, and the only torment of Ellis's that was visible was his embarrassment over having been exposed by the *Boston Globe*. That argument was not only speculative; it was silly.

Her most important argument was the line "in his work, if not in his life, Ellis has never crossed the line between fiction and history."

Of course for a professor, lecturing in the classroom is indeed "work." But this argument can only mean one thing: lying to students is a minor offense as long as he didn't "lie" to readers. He lied in the classroom but told the truth in his books—and the latter is what's important. What you say to readers counts; what you say to students doesn't really matter. That's the key argument Shulevitz made in the *New York Times Book Review.*

The next month, after Mount Holyoke had sent Ellis on an unpaid year off, the editors of the *New York Times* made pretty much the same argument. They noted that the penalty "amounts, after all, to an unwanted, unpaid sabbatical with continued office and library privileges." This was "fair" and "appropriate," given the nature of the offense, but nevertheless regrettable. Ellis's lies to students were "sadly self-defeating"—but, the *Times* failed to note, only because he got caught. The editorial lapsed into psychologizing: "Why should a man as successful as Mr. Ellis . . . feel compelled to reinvent his past?" The *Times* editors had an answer: in lying to students, he was "projecting his current degree of success backward in time, living up to a version of himself." This tragic flaw made it possible to understand, and thus forgive, Ellis. Students expect teachers to be truthful in class; but "for the vast majority of his tenure Mr. Ellis lived up to that expectation, in just the ways he should have. What the college classroom requires is the best a professor can bring to it. Mr. Ellis clearly felt that his best was not good enough." The end.[30] Thus the *New York Times* editorial ended with sympathy and understanding for Ellis and his feelings—rather than sympathy for the students whose trust he betrayed.

Full exoneration came in March 2002, just nine months after the scandal broke, when the *New York Times Book Review* ran a piece by Ellis on a new Jefferson book. The ID line for the reviewer made it clear that the paper was willing to forgive and forget—and did not want to remind its readers what had happened at Mount Holyoke. Before the scandal, Ellis had been identified in the reviews he wrote for the *Times* not only as the author of his Jefferson book, but also as "the Ford Foundation Professor of American History at Mount Holyoke College." His new, post-scandal ID did not mention the scene of his offense: it read simply "Joseph J. Ellis is the author of *Founding Brothers: The Revolutionary Generation.*"[31]

11

The Plagiarists: Doris Kearns Goodwin and Stephen Ambrose

Most of the historians in trouble over the last few years have been charged with plagiarism. It's the easiest kind of academic misconduct to document, and the easiest for the public to understand—everybody knows copying somebody else's work and claiming it's your own is wrong. And when a newspaper article or a TV news magazine puts texts by two authors side by side and shows they are the same, the case is closed.

Side-by-side comparisons published in 2002 showed that Doris Kearns Goodwin's 1987 book *The Fitzgeralds and the Kennedys* had incorporated several passages from Lynne McTaggart's 1983 book, *Kathleen Kennedy: Her Life and Times*. Goodwin had won the Pulitzer Prize in 1995 for her book *No Ordinary Time* about Franklin and Eleanor Roosevelt.

But Goodwin had done more than plagiarize—she had paid the writer from whom she had plagiarized a "substantial" amount in exchange for secrecy about it. This deal succeeded in keeping the plagiarism secret for fifteen years. When the deal finally became public in 2002, Goodwin explained that "the whole understanding was supposed to be confidential just because of the nature of it."[1]

In response to evidence first published in the *Weekly Standard* in January 2002, Goodwin admitted that McTaggart had complained to her about the plagiarism shortly after the book's publication in 1987; Goodwin's publisher and attorneys then negotiated an agreement in which she paid McTaggart a "substantial" sum in exchange for McTaggart's silence about the plagiarism.

After the deal became public, McTaggart wrote an op-ed piece for the *New York Times* explaining what had happened: "I discovered [Goodwin's plagiarism] in the course of doing a review of Ms. Goodwin's book. I was shocked to read passage after passage of my own book embedded in hers. *I wrote a kind review* [italics added], then hired a copyright lawyer. We eventually reached a satisfactory settlement." Timothy Noah of *Slate* was pretty much the only writer on the story to explain what McTaggart had done: "hide the book's flaws in public, squeeze the book's author for cash in private."[2]

When the scandal first broke, McTaggart had refused to comment, sticking to the confidentiality agreement. Her first public statement came in late January 2002, telling the *Weekly Standard* that she had "no regrets" over the confidential settlement of her complaint. "I respected the fact that [Goodwin] had a reputation to protect," she said. "I don't want to destroy her reputation or have her book considered worthless."[3]

The secret settlement, according to Bo Crader of the *Weekly Standard,* also included an agreement by Goodwin to add forty new endnotes citing McTaggart in a new edition, along with a statement in the preface to the new edition that McTaggart's book "is the definitive biography of Kathleen Kennedy . . . which I used as a primary source for information on Kathleen Kennedy, both in my research and in my writing." Although the preface to the first edition did not mention McTaggart, Crader pointed out, "the dateline of the preface in both editions reads "November 1986"—concealing the fact of Goodwin's plagiarism.[4]

Nixon's rule—"the cover-up is always worse than the crime"— did not apply to the Goodwin case. Virtually all the discussion in the press focused on the plagiarism and somehow ignored the more serious fact that Goodwin had paid to keep the plagiarism secret. In her public statements, Goodwin argued repeatedly that she was not guilty of plagiarism—despite the evidence from side-by-side comparisons—just sloppy research, "mistakes," and "errors."[5] She got high-level support in a letter to the editor published by the *New York Times,* signed by Arthur Schlesinger Jr., Douglas Brinkley, Robert Dallek, and David Halberstam. The letter read, "We write as historians to attest to our high regard for the scholarship and integrity of Doris Kearns Goodwin and to protest vigorously your article 'Are More People Cheating?' with the photograph of Ms. Goodwin displayed in the company of some of the most notorious scoundrels in America." The writers defined plagiarism as "a deliberate intent to purloin the words of another and to represent them as one's own," and argued that Goodwin's "errors resulted from inadvertence, not intent." "She did not, she does not, cheat or plagiarize.

In fact, her character and work symbolize the highest standards of moral integrity." The History News Network published the names of additional signers, who included John M. Blum, John Diggins, and Sean Wilentz.[6] The distinguished historians who publicly praised Goodwin for her "moral integrity" had somehow overlooked the deal in which she paid "a substantial sum" to keep her plagiarism secret.

The *New York Times* revealed that Goodwin was working with a political consultant, Robert Shrum, to line up support for her defense in the media. She appeared on the David Letterman show—the only historian accused of misconduct ever to do so—and, according to the *Times,* she had also gotten Senator Ted Kennedy, a friend, to intervene on her behalf. The *Times* then quoted Princeton historian and former AHA president Robert Darnton: "If she is organizing a P.R. campaign to exculpate herself, that strikes me as unprofessional conduct."[7]

Goodwin paid a price for plagiarizing: she was forced to resign from the Pulitzer Prize committee, and she gave up her position as a commentator on the *MacNeil-Lehrer News Hour* on PBS. But her banishment didn't last long. By 2004, NBC-TV News had hired her as a "news analyst" and she was appearing as a political commentator on *Hardball* with Chris Matthews, CNBC News, and on *Meet the Press* alongside such heavyweights as William Safire, David Broder, and Robert Novak.[8]

In the case of Doris Kearns Goodwin, the cover-up wasn't worse than the crime—the cover-up was forgotten. She paid a price for her plagiarism, she and her defenders mounted a media campaign to restore her good name, and it succeeded.

*   *   *

Goodwin was famous when she got into trouble, but the *Chronicle of Higher Education* intermittently carries reports of little-known academics and university administrators who were disciplined or even fired by their institutions for plagiarism. A few random recent examples: in November 2003, the U.S. Naval Academy found historian Brian VanDeMark guilty of plagiarism in his book about the development of the atomic bomb; he was stripped of tenure and had his salary cut by $10,000. The president of Hamilton College, Eugene Tobin, resigned in 2002 after admitting he used plagiarized material in speeches over the previous nine years; his speech to freshmen the previous fall, on books he had read over the summer, had included material published on the Amazon.com website. Louis W. Roberts, chair of the classics department at SUNY-Albany, was stripped of his chairmanship after being found guilty of plagiarizing "large portions" of his book *Latin Texts from the First Century B.C. to the Seventh Century A.D.*[9]

The late Stephen Ambrose is the best-known historian charged with plagiarism. His story is an extreme one—both in the number of sources from which he plagiarized, and in the immense success of the author—but it illuminates some key issues: the characteristic terms of accusation and modes of response and the ways the history profession engages the issues. Ambrose, the author of more than twenty books, gained wealth and fame for several histories of World War II, featuring strong narratives and vivid characters. More than any other historian, he created—and profited from—the "greatest generation" phenomenon. His book *Band of Brothers* became a ten-part series on HBO with a budget of $125 million. The peak moment for Ambrose probably came in 2000 with the opening of the D-day museum he founded in his home town of New Orleans, where he shared the stage with Tom Hanks and Stephen Spielberg; Ambrose had been an official consultant on their film *Saving Private Ryan,* and they produced the HBO miniseries based on his book.[10]

Ambrose had first gained attention with a respected three-volume authorized biography of Eisenhower that took him twenty years to write, which was followed by a well-received two-volume biography of Nixon on which he spent ten years. But the turning point in his career came when he was sixty years old, in 1994, with the book *D-Day, June 6, 1944: The Climactic Battle of World War II*. The book spent more than thirty weeks on the bestseller list. After the D-day book, Ambrose published a dozen more, at a rate of more than one a year. Eventually, he sold over five million books. The *Wall Street Journal* described him as "Stephen Ambrose Inc., an extraordinarily successful business that conducts historical research, supports museums, produces and markets books, and negotiates movie deals."[11]

Ambrose Inc. also ran historical tours. An ad reproduced by the History News Network read, "Join the Stephen Ambrose Italian Campaign Tour, April 17–28 NEW! From Stephen Ambrose Historical Tours—The Italian Campaign Tour—April 17–28, 2002. This unique tour designed by historian Stephen E. Ambrose follows in the footsteps of General Mark Clark and the American 5th Army during the pivotal 1944–45 battles in Italy. The extraordinary 11-day, 9-night tour is led by Twenty-Five Yards of War author and retired USMC Captain Ron Drez. Visit www.StephenAmbroseTours. com or call today: (888) 903-3329." The *Journal* estimated that the Ambrose family operation was making $3 million a year.[12]

Then, in January 2002, the *Weekly Standard* broke the story of Ambrose's plagiarism. Fred Barnes reported that Ambrose's newest bestseller, *The Wild Blue,* a book about bomber pilots in World War II that featured the heroism of George McGovern, contained several passages that were identical to passages in Thomas Childers's book *Wings of Morning: The Story of the Last American Bomber Shot Down over Germany in World War II.*[13]

Only two days after the charges were published, Ambrose issued an apology: "I made a mistake for which I am sorry," he said in a statement released by his publisher to the *New York Times.* He promised to put the plagiarized passages in quotation marks "in future editions of the book." Barnes responded with praise for the speedy and unqualified apology. He offered his own semi-exoneration, explaining that Ambrose probably slipped up in the rush to publication. And he concluded by recommending Ambrose's books to readers.[14] That seemed like the end of it. The media, and the public, like a forthright and straightforward apology, which they regard as the necessary step to the happy ending called "closure."

But the same day Ambrose apologized, *Forbes* posted a piece on its website claiming that, way back in his 1975 book *Crazy Horse and Custer,* Ambrose had plagiarized from Jay Monaghan's 1959 book, *Custer: The Life of General George Armstrong Custer.* A couple of days later, Forbes.com claimed that two other Ambrose books contained plagiarized passages: *Citizen Soldiers* and *Nixon: Ruin and*

Recovery 1973–1990. A couple of days after that, the *New York Times* showed that *The Wild Blue* contained passages that had been plagiarized from two additional books, Michael Sherry's *The Rise of American Air Power* and *The Army Air Force in World War II,* edited by Wesley F. Craven and J.L. Cate. Later in February, Forbes.com was back with an even more damning report that in *The Wild Blue* Ambrose had plagiarized from six additional books, including the memoir of George McGovern.[15] That was the evidence, and it seemed indisputable.

Then came the defense. The first argument for the defense was that Ambrose was a good man. That argument came from McGovern himself, who wrote in a letter to the *New York Times* that Ambrose "is not only a superb historian, but also a gifted writer whose books are devoured by the public, and a patriot who has donated millions of dollars to environmental and educational causes." "He is one of the few great men I have been privileged to know," McGovern concluded.[16]

The second line of defense was that the plagiarism was insignificant. Ambrose himself made that argument in a letter to the *Wall Street Journal,* complaining about an op-ed piece by Mark Lewis: "He writes that my 'plagiarism is not limited to a few sentences,' but fails to point out the real amount—is it 10 sentences? 15? 20?—or to mention that my books have about 50 footnotes per chapter, or some 1,000 per book, making a total of perhaps 24,000 footnotes. He fails to mention that I have published hundreds of thousands of sentences."

The third defense was that Ambrose was actually innocent. Richard Jensen, an emeritus professor at the University of Illinois,

Chicago, made this argument in the *OAH Newsletter*. He quoted the American Historical Association Statement on Plagiarism, and then declared, "I have looked at all their allegations, and not one meets the AHA test." Ambrose never "tried to deceive the audience or falsify evidence," he argued. *Forbes* had charged that Ambrose plagiarized Cornelius Ryan's work: "False," Jensen wrote; "Ambrose did not use a single word of Ryan's." *Forbes* had charged that Ambrose plagiarized Jay Monaghan's description of Custer's arrival at West Point, but "both Ambrose and Monaghan used the same words taken from the same primary source."[17]

Finally, in February Ambrose posted a response to critics on his website, StephenAmbrose.com: "Recently I have been criticized for improperly attributing other authors' writings in a few of my books. In each case, I footnoted the passage in question, but failed to put some words and sentences into quotation marks. I am sorry for those omissions, and will make relevant changes in all future editions of my books. I would also like to thank all of you who have written in to express your friendship and support."[18] He then announced that he would write only one more book—a history of the war in the Pacific—and devote the rest of his life to environmental work.[19]

That was February 2002. Ambrose published another defense at his website in May, claiming that the plagiarized material—he used the term "copied words" instead—amounted to only "10 pages out of a total work of some 15,000 pages in print," and he promised to insert the necessary quotation marks in "all future editions." The same month he told the *Los Angeles Times* that, because of his advanced lung cancer, he was abandoning the World War II book to write a memoir, titled "A Love Song to America." Asked about the charges of plagiarism, he had one comment: "Screw it." He said he wanted to focus on finishing his memoir, and "If they decide I'm a fraud, I'm a fraud. I don't know that I'm all that good at academics. I'm a writer."[20] He died of lung cancer eight months later.

His death provided the occasion for a public summing up of the significance of the charges against him. The obituary in the *Washington Post* referred only briefly to the scandal: "Some feel that jealousy helped lead to the bump in Dr. Ambrose's writing career this year when accusations of plagiarism were raised against him." The *Post* concluded that the offense was minor: "It turned out that while questioned passages in a couple of books lacked quotation marks, the quotes were footnoted." The *Post* then cited an authority, Arthur Schlesinger Jr., who praised Ambrose for his "high standards of scholarship."[21]

The obit in the *New York Times* was only slightly more critical: "Mr. Ambrose said that his copying from other writers' works represented only a few pages among the thousands he had written and that he had identified the sources by providing footnotes. He did concede that he should have placed quotation marks around such material and said he would do so in future editions. He denied engaging in plagiarism."[22]

The charges against Ambrose were never adjudicated by any academic institution or professional body. The AHA had issued a revised policy statement on plagiarism in 2002, declaring that universities needed to follow procedures that were "organized and punitive." It was first of all the responsibility of "the employing institution" to "investigate charges of plagiarism promptly and impartially and to invoke appropriate sanctions when the charges are sustained." Cases of "a persistent pattern of deception" could justify "termination of an academic career."[23]

The AHA also had its own body charged with adjudicating charges of plagiarism—a five-person elected "Professional Division," established in 1974. The Professional Division regularly conducted investigations and issued reports in previous cases of plagiarism, most notably that of Lincoln biographer Stephen Oates. However, its proceedings were "confidential from the time of initial inquiry until the complaint is resolved," as one chairperson explained, and "the AHA publicizes its findings only in exceptional circumstances." Professional adjudication by the AHA aimed at the private resolution of disputes between two authors rather than the public evaluation of charges.[24]

Ambrose was denied the privilege of secluded adjudication of the charges against him, Ron Robin writes in his book *Scandals and Scoundrels,* because of his "celebrity." But he wasn't "denied" a professional forum—in fact, nobody brought a complaint against Ambrose before the AHA. Jackson Lears, a prominent historian at Rutgers, declared at the height of the scandal that, if Ambrose were still a "tenured professor, his university career would have been ended by this"—but since he had retired from the University of New Orleans to run Ambrose Inc. full time, that university had no standing to investigate and punish him.[25]

Because plagiarism itself is intellectually uninteresting, writers on the topic have sought to find larger meanings in cases like Ambrose's.

Ron Robin argues that the Ambrose case was one where plagiarism served as "the pretext for debating issues of far greater cultural complexity" than literary larceny, where "political and intellectual subtexts" provided the real significance of the scandal. The plagiarism scandal, he argues, ignited a broad criticism of Ambrose on issues "above and beyond" unattributed citations.[26]

Robin cites Nicholas Confessore's critique "Selling Private Ryan" as one of the most important of these works. Confessore criticized Ambrose for "a profoundly distorted view of America at war." Ambrose, he wrote, failed to give credit to Britain or the USSR for fighting mostly alone against Hitler in the crucial opening years of the war. He mistakenly described the Normandy invasion as "the climactic battle of World War II," and the war itself as a "test of national systems" in "which democracy proved better able to produce young men who could be made into superb soldiers than Nazi Germany." In fact, Stalingrad had marked the decisive turning point in the European war, which suggested—in Ambrose's terms—that Stalinism "proved better able" to defeat Hitler. Moreover, Confessore argued, Ambrose's books rested almost exclusively on interviews conducted decades after the events in question, but Ambrose failed to question the status of memory or to test it against other kinds of sources. Finally, Confessore argued, "He neither raises nor attempts to settle any questions of historical importance."[27]

A second key critique of Ambrose's work cited by Ron Robin was Benjamin Schwarz's essay in the *Atlantic,* where Ambrose's work was described as a "simplistic and sanctimonious" effort that "evades the truth." American soldiers on the Normandy beaches in Ambrose's account were fighting for decency and democracy—but

Schwarz argues that nobody who has studied soldiers in battle thinks they fight for such "abstract, imprecise, and gaseous sentiments." Ambrose says American troops on D-day were motivated by a desire to free France from Nazi tyranny and put a stop to the Holocaust—but, Schwarz argues, the purpose of the Normandy invasion was simply to defeat the Nazi army, and America's official propaganda never mentioned the Holocaust. He quotes Paul Fussell arguing that most Americans supported the war to get revenge against the Japanese: "The slogan was conspicuously 'Remember Pearl Harbor.' No one ever shouted or sang 'Remember Poland.' "[28]

Ron Robin cites Confessore and Schwarz as evidence that the plagiarism scandal "ignited a broad criticism" of Ambrose's methods and conclusions. But both Confessore and Schwarz published their critiques well before the plagiarism scandal broke in January 2002. Confessore's article appeared in the *American Prospect* in September 2001, and Schwarz's appeared in the *Atlantic* even before that, in June 2001—seven months before the first plagiarism scandals appeared. The key intellectual and historical criticism of Ambrose preceded the plagiarism scandal, rather than being "ignited" by it.

Ron Robin makes a second argument: the force that drove the Ambrose case, he argues, was not just the desire to expose scholarly wrongdoing, but more importantly a passion to criticize "celebrity historians" precisely for their "hybridity"—for "the fusion and attendant confusion of an intellectual calling with popular writing." The real charge against Ambrose, in this view, was not that he stole others' words, but that he mixed genres—that he crossed "the fine

line dividing intellectual activity from sentimental boosterism,"
that he engaged in "facile hero-worshipping."[29]

The evidence for this argument is weak. It's true that writers on
the left criticized Ambrose for his celebration of patriotism and his
military triumphalism, which ignored, among other things, the
Vietnam experience.

But the campaign against Ambrose's plagiarism—as opposed to
his historical interpretation—didn't come from the left, from critics
of "boosterism" and "facile hero-worshipping"; it came from the
right: from the *Weekly Standard* and from Forbes.com—from sources
that shared Ambrose's patriotic boosterism and hero-worshipping of
the military. Those complaints came in the stern voice of traditional
values and were all about honesty and truthfulness in citations.
In this case, the left—in the *American Prospect* and the *Atlantic*—
criticized Ambrose on intellectual and historical grounds, and then
the right—the *Weekly Standard* and Forbes.com—criticized him for
plagiarism.

Although neither Ambrose nor Goodwin received the secluded adjudication that the AHA offered others accused of plagiarism, the
AHA procedure was deeply flawed. The case of Jayme Sokolow, reported by Thomas Mallon in his wonderful book *Stolen Words,* provides a dramatic example of the problem. In 1981, Sokolow was
being considered for tenure in the history department at Texas Tech
in Lubbock. Among the materials he submitted as part of his
tenure file was his book manuscript, which he had submitted to

several university presses. The manuscript included a large portion
of the doctoral dissertation of Stephen Nissenbaum, a distinguished
historian of early America teaching at U. Mass Amherst, which had
been published as *Sex, Diet, and Debility in Jacksonian America* (Nissenbaum is best known as the co-author of *Salem Possessed,* a prize-
winning study of witchcraft). Since Sokolow's manuscript was in
Nissenbaum's field, the presses asked him to review Sokolow's manuscript. Nissenbaum recognized his own work, and informed the
presses and also Texas Tech that the manuscript was plagiarized; he
also informed the AHA Professional Division. Sokolow responded
by admitting only "sloppy notetaking," but he resigned from Texas
Tech without facing a tenure vote. And the presses all rejected the
manuscript.[30]

Unfortunately, as Thomas Mallon shows, the story did not end
there. Because the AHA Professional Division did not make its
findings public, that organization made no public statement about
Sokolow's plagiarism. Texas Tech never said publicly that he had
resigned because his book manuscript had been plagiarized. None
of the university presses that rejected made any public statement
explaining why.[31]

As a result, Nissenbaum explained to Mallon, "Sokolow went on
as if nothing had happened." He continued to submit the plagiarized
manuscript to other publishers, and eventually, in 1983, Farleigh
Dickinson University Press published it: *Eros and Modernization:
Sylvester Graham, Health Reform, and the Origins of Victorian Sexuality in
America*. Twenty years later, the book is probably in every research library in the country; for example, the University of California library
catalogue shows the book is in the libraries at Berkeley, UCLA,

Davis, Irvine, Riverside, Santa Barbara, Santa Cruz, San Diego and San Francisco—every campus in the system. In 1987, Sokolow submitted a second plagiarized manuscript for publication. Even more amazing, he got a job as a program officer at the National Endowment for the Humanities, where he worked for five years monitoring the research grants awarded to scholars.[32]

Nissenbaum blames the American Historical Association for failing to expose Sokolow as a plagiarist. When Nissenbaum first wrote the AHA in 1984, Otto Pflanze, editor of the official AHA journal, the *American Historical Review* (*AHR*) suggested Nissenbaum file a complaint with the Professional Division of the organization. Rather than do that himself, Nissenbaum persuaded his department chairman, Robert Griffith, to draft a complaint, documenting the plagiarism—it ended up fifteen pages long.[33]

Even after the AHA leadership had overwhelming evidence that Sokolow had committed plagiarism, the *AHR* did not publish any statement or review about it. Instead, AHA Executive Director Samuel Gammon negotiated with Sokolow about what the *AHR* would say about his offenses. The *AHR,* edited at the time by Otto Pflanze, eventually agreed to run a long letter of Sokolow's under the heading "Professional Matters." In it, Sokolow did not admit that his book had substantial similarities to Nissenbaum's dissertation; instead, he wrote, "I studied closely Professor Nissenbaum's fine dissertation prior to the writing of my own book. . . . Belated acknowledgment has been put into an Errata that accompanies my book, and I urge any reviewers and readers to study the emendations carefully."[34] Those who wrote to the publisher requesting the errata slip found that it did not admit to plagiarism, but instead contains footnotes to ninety-two pages of Nissenbaum's book and to an additional thirty-three pages of the dissertation on which the book had been based. In his errata slip, Sokolow had the chutzpah to compliment Nissenbaum for his "pioneering," "excellent," and "fine" research.[35]

Nissenbaum was outraged that the *AHR* published Sokolow's misleading letter. Still he did not comment in print. Instead, he wrote in a private letter to the AHA Professional Division, "Sokolow has implicitly claimed his book will henceforth be a legitimate work of scholarship. And by agreeing to Sokolow's wording, and his Errata, the AHA has accepted his definition of the problem." The deputy executive director of the AHA, Jamil S. Zainaldin, replied to Nissenbaum that this was "the best resolution" of the issue "short of litigation."[36]

The year after the *AHR* published Sokolow's deceptive statement, the AHA published a "Statement on Plagiarism," drafted by the Professional Division in part on the basis of their experience with Sokolow. The statement proclaimed that a "persistent pattern" of deception "justifies a termination of an academic career," and that findings of the Professional Division regarding plagiarism "should ordinarily be made public."[37]

The victim of Sokolow's second plagiarized manuscript filed a complaint in 1987 with the AHA Professional Division under its new and forthright "Statement on Plagiarism." Sokolow's repeated submissions of the plagiarized manuscript certainly constituted what the "Statement" had defined as a "persistent pattern." Although the division agreed that the manuscript had been plagiarized, it decided to keep both the complaint and its findings secret. Thus it protected

Sokolow from exposure even though it found him guilty. This policy permitted Sokolow to continue to submit his second plagiarized manuscript to publishers, and to get it accepted and advertised as "forthcoming" in 1989. (It never appeared.)

Finally in 1990 Nissenbaum published an article about his experience. In the *Chronicle of Higher Education* he pointed out that "two universities, at least seven publishing houses, and three major national organizations all knew of Sokolow's misconduct"; yet "to this day not one of them . . . has openly condemned what he did."[38] The only person to write about the Sokolow case had been Thomas Mallon in *Stolen Words*.

AHA officials had told Nissenbaum the reason for their silence was fear of a libel suit. But the best defense against libel is truth, and the truth is that Sokolow had plagiarized. Thomas Mallon's publisher, Ticknor & Fields, clearly had confidence in the truth of his book: the Sokolow chapter is massively documented, with seven pages of notes citing interviews with ten people and quoting from numerous pieces of private correspondence. In addition, Sokolow's former colleagues at Texas Tech also went public, providing documentation and permitting Mallon to quote them in his book. They viewed Mallon's requests for interviews not as posing a potential problem of litigation, but rather as providing an opportunity to tell the public the truth.

Thus, there's a striking contrast in this case between the official leaders of the profession, who failed to demonstrate the courage and commitment to make public the truth about Sokolow's plagiarism, and those who did. Those who failed included the executive director of the American Historical Association, Samuel Gammon, and the editor of the *American Historical Review* at the time, Otto Pflanze. The historians at Texas Tech failed to contact Nissenbaum or the publisher, but in the end several at Tech (John Wunder, Otto Nelson, Jim Brink, Allan Keuthe, Jeffrey Smitten, Jacquelin Collins, and Benjamin Newcomb) told the story to Thomas Mallon. Credit goes most of all to Mallon, at the time a lecturer in English at Vassar College.[39] Nissenbaum himself could have gone public at the beginning, but didn't, he says, because he hoped the profession would defend him. He was wrong.

Conclusion

The *William and Mary Quarterly* (*WMQ*) published two "Forums" in its January 2002 issue—the first a series of articles that debated problems in Edward Pearson's book about Denmark Vesey, while the second debated problems in Michael Bellesiles's book *Arming America*. The Vesey book was shown to have transcription errors on virtually every page, and more seriously, a deeply erroneous description of the document at the center of the book: it was not, as Pearson described it, a verbatim "trial transcript," but rather a retrospective summary of testimony for the prosecution, revised by persons unknown to us. This misunderstanding, in the view of many, undermined the author's entire thesis. Shortly after publication of the critique in the *WMQ*, the publisher withdrew the book. Nevertheless, the fatal problems with the Vesey book received virtually no media attention, nor were there any moves in the history profession to investigate or discipline Pearson; his college decided to take no disciplinary action—apparently because the scholarly criticism and the publisher's action were deemed sufficient. Pearson remains chair of the department at his college.

Bellesiles of course had the opposite fate. After the massive media event around his book came to an end, he published a second revised edition of his book, correcting errors in the first, but as of this writing (summer 2004), he no longer has a faculty position at a college or university.

Thus some historians in trouble have had their careers ended, while others received little or no attention or punishment. In still other cases, like those of Elizabeth Fox-Genovese, Allen Weinstein, and Stephan Thernstrom, the offenders have been rewarded—with White House nominations—after their troubles were spun by the right-wing media as "standing up to political correctness"—or, in the case of Weinstein, simply ignored. Of course, it's standard political practice for the president to make appointments based on appointees' support for his positions—but it's also legitimate to raise questions about whether nominees' past conduct makes them appropriate appointees for Archivist of the United States or members of the board of the National Endowment for the Humanities.

There is no single lesson to be found or meaning to be discovered in the twelve cases examined in this book. In the cases of the historians targeted by the right—Michael Bellesiles, David Abraham, and Mike Davis—the critics' tactic was to highlight small errors as a way of denying much broader and more significant truths. Bellesiles's problematic Table 1, which led to his downfall, in fact was referred to only a couple of times in a 400-page book on the origins of gun culture in America. The errors in David Abraham's note-taking did not affect the validity of his interpretation of the collapse of the Weimar Republic. And the small number of flaws in Mike Davis's footnotes did not undermine his argument connecting long-term environmental history with short-term decisions by the powerful. Instead of making arguments against interpretations they disagreed with, critics focused on minor discrepancies in the documentation in each case—and concealed their political disagreements behind vociferous charges of "fraud."

There are some additional lessons:

The lesson of the David Abraham case (aside from "take good notes") seems to be "don't write a dissertation that challenges powerful people in your field, especially if you are on the left and they are on the right." The lesson of the Mike Davis case (aside from "take good notes") is that it's possible to survive a damaging media attack—at least if you have won a MacArthur "genius" grant, a Getty fellowship, and some book prizes. The lesson of the Joseph Ellis case seems to be that the *New York Times* and the *New Yorker* will forgive you for lying about history—as long as you told your lies to students rather than readers. The lesson of the Dino Cinel case seems to be that you can't lie about sexual abuse of young people and keep your teaching job—even if the AFT defends you.

One of the lessons here is that some of the most serious cases of misconduct have not received the most serious sanctions. Indeed, sanctions have been severe only where pressure groups with political agendas have organized campaigns demanding punishment. In the case of Bellesiles, the demands that he be fired for his errors, that his book be withdrawn, and that his prize be rescinded, came not from historians at colleges or universities, but rather from organized gun rights advocates. University administrators and trustees have little to gain by standing up to organized groups promising continuing bad publicity and threats to fund-raising.

Obviously this is not a good way to resolve charges of misconduct. The academy, and the history profession, needs an alternative. A strong and independent profession might be able to stand up to the pressure of organized political groups with their own agendas—might be able to provide some counterweight for administrators facing pressure from outside.

Can the American Historical Association be that kind of strong and independent force? The AHA announced in May 2003 that, after fifteen years of investigations and reports aimed at enforcing the profession's "Statement on Standards of Professional Conduct," it was giving up the effort. It would no longer investigate and adjudicate complaints.[1]

The current AHA "Statement on Standards" covers many issues in addition to plagiarism: "access to sources"—the issue in the Allen Weinstein case; "integrity" in research—an issue for John Lott; "civility," and "fairness" in hiring and employment practices—both relevant to the case of Elizabeth Fox-Genovese and to the conduct of Gerald Feldman and Henry Turner in the David Abraham case.[2]

The decision to abandon AHA enforcement of the "Statement on Standards" had been pushed by William J. Cronon, a professor of history at the University of Wisconsin-Madison, who at the time served as head of the Professional Division. At that point, he said, the division had been receiving "50 to 100 inquiries annually," and conducting formal investigations of misconduct in about ten cases a year.

The key problem that led to the AHA's decision was the requirement of confidentiality in both investigating complaints and announcing decisions. As a result, Cronon explained, AHA investigations "had virtually no public impact on the profession." "For the most part, only those who complained or were complained against knew the outcome of complaints. Adjudication has not promoted a wide public and professional understanding of what historians mean by scholarly integrity," he explained. Instead of maintaining confidentiality, Cronon wrote, the best response to charges of misconduct would be to replace the AHA procedures with "public debate."[3]

But of course Cronon and the AHA Professional Division could have contributed to that public debate—not by abandoning the adjudication of charges of misconduct, but instead by making their findings public.

The second reason the AHA abandoned adjudication of complaints stemmed from the fact that the AHA had no power to impose sanctions. As a result, Cronon said, its rulings seemed meaningless. "We would send two letters, one to the person who was accused and the other to the person who made the accusation," Cronon told the *Chronicle of Higher Education*. "That's it. How can you run a court that doesn't have any power to punish?"[4] The power to punish lay with the colleges and universities that employed the offenders, Cronon argued, and it was their responsibility to act. He pointed to Emory's actions in the Bellesiles case as a good example.

But if the AHA's proceedings and decisions in cases of misconduct were public, the AHA report could conclude with a call on the universities that employed the offending scholars to fulfill the requirements of the AHA "Statement on Standards" and discipline and punish the guilty.[5]

Professional adjudication of charges of misconduct is no panacea. The AHA in the past has made some poor decisions. Its procedures have been secretive and cumbersome, its leaders and officials have sometimes been cowardly or worse. But who else has the standing and the expertise to resist organized pressure groups? Public adjudication of charges of misconduct by the AHA, including discussion of appropriate penalties, may not produce good results. But without the AHA, it's likely to be worse. University administrators will only be weaker and more vulnerable in the face of organized political groups seeking to impose their partisan agendas on the academy.

While the AHA Professional Division threw in the towel, the editors of the *American Historical Review* moved in the opposite direction, taking on more responsibility for policing misconduct. The medium there is the book review. Should reviewers raise questions about plagiarism or research fraud if they suspect an author? The previous book review guidelines for the *AHR* said nothing, except for a vague and discouraging statement noting, "We do delete passages that are, in our judgment, *ad hominem* attacks on an author." The new guidelines, adopted in 2003, added to that sentence the following statements:

These include unsubstantiated or libelous allegations of plagiarism. However, we also accept the responsibility to publish responsible charges of misappropriated scholarship. Such claims must be documented with examples of parallel texts or of instances of the unattributed use of other scholars' ideas and arguments. Such judgments are made in accordance with our fundamental responsibility to promote the freest possible discussion of the articles and reviews published in the *AHR* and our responsibility to uphold the American Historical Association's Standards of Professional Conduct, which require all historians to maintain "the highest standards of intellectual integrity" and to evaluate "the honesty and reliability with which the historian uses primary and secondary source material."[6]

The new policy applies also to letters to the editors about book reviews, where charges of plagiarism and research fraud may also appear.

AHR editor Michael Grossberg explained that the change was intended specifically to empower book reviewers to bring charges of misconduct before the public—precisely what the Professional Division decided the AHA should not do. Now it will be the journal editors instead of the AHA committee members who will decide whether charges are legitimate.

Grossberg explained that the biggest concern in adopting the new policy was "the fiduciary responsibilities of editors . . . to their journal." He stated with refreshing frankness the real anxiety: "If we broadcast such a finding, will we be subject to a suit for libel?" The problem, he explained, is that "fear of libel suits hovers over the entire subject of plagiarism," because the consequences for the accused are so serious. Richard Posner explained it: "The label 'plagiarist' can ruin a writer, destroy a scholarly career, blast a politician's chances for reelection, and cause the expulsion of a student from a college or university."[7] The same could be said about other forms of scholarly misconduct.

Why are the editors of the *AHR* willing to face libel litigation? Grossberg answered that question with wonderful clarity: "We cannot let such fears prevent us from meeting our obligations; instead, we must devise reasonable, defensible, and effective policies that allow us to do so."[8] It is noteworthy that Grossberg, in addition to serving as editor of the *AHR,* is also a professor of law.

Understanding historians in trouble requires looking not just inside the profession, at its policies and procedures, but also outside—at larger forces in the culture and the media. Historians in trouble need to be put in perspective, as Elliot Gorn has suggested: recent corporate fraud has involved billions of dollars, the Catholic Church has covered up sexual abuse of children by thousands of priests, and the president took the country to war on the basis of lies about Iraqi weapons of mass destruction and links between Saddam Hussein and Osama bin Laden.[9] Compared to these developments, the recent troubles involving historians are insignificant.

But perhaps they are not unrelated; perhaps, as David Callahan has argued recently, the historians in trouble and the indicted CEOs are all part of the same "cheating culture." The Reagan Revolution enshrined the market as the highest measure of value in our society, Callahan argues, and the result has been a glorification of money and success at the expense of "old-fashioned ideas about fairness." It has also resulted in an increasing income gap between the very wealthy and everybody else, a gap that has brought new pressures that make ordinary people more anxious about their financial security and more willing to take part in "trickle-down corruption"—the widespread belief that you're unlikely to get caught and punished for cheating.[10]

Callahan's "cheating culture" website (www.CheatingCulture.com) has a section devoted to historians—Ambrose, Bellesiles, Goodwin, and two others are listed—after the sections on corporations (Enron et al.) and accounting firms (like Arthur Anderson, which helped Enron's multibillion dollar fraud). The similarities seem limited, mostly because of the immense scale of scandals like Enron's. But there is a crucial common point: historians do not work in ivory towers; they compete in markets like everybody else, as Elliot Gorn points out: "job markets, tenure markets, publishing markets—places where competition allocates scarce resources."[11]

"Trickle-down corruption" might describe two on Callahan's list of cheating historians: Brian VanDeMark, the tenured professor at the Naval Academy whose book *Pandora's Keepers: Nine Men and the Atomic Bomb* included over thirty plagiarized passages, and Louis Roberts, the chair of Classics at SUNY-Albany, who plagiarized fifty pages of Latin translations. Callahan and Gorn could argue that VanDeMark's and Roberts's plagiarism resembles the cheating of ordinary employees who lie to get a promotion after reading about Enron's tax dodges.

Callahan also has Michael Bellesiles on his list of cheating historians. But the errors that ruined Bellesiles's career, like those of

David Abraham, are different from the trickle-down cheating of the plagiarists. It's worth recalling how Lawrence Stone, talking about David Abraham, described the problem of error: "When you work in the archives," he said, "you're far from home, you're bored, you're in a hurry, you're scribbling like crazy. You're bound to make mistakes. I don't believe any scholar in the Western world has impeccable footnotes. Archival research is a special case of the general messiness of life."[12]

The "cheating culture" argument explains scholarly misconduct as the result of a calculus in which the potential benefits resulting from dishonesty are seen to be great and the chances of paying a penalty, small. That certainly proved to be the case for John Lott and for Allen Weinstein. Lott continues to publish op-eds in prestigious venues despite the deception in his book on guns; Allen Weinstein was nominated by President Bush to be Archivist of the United States, despite his refusal—for twenty-five years—to document that he did not misquote key interviewees.

These two cases, however, share a distinctive feature: both Lott and Weinstein work outside the university. Neither has an academic position. Neither is subject to faculty disciplinary proceedings of the kind that Joseph Ellis and Michael Bellesiles and Edward Pearson faced. Lott and Weinstein both worked for private think tanks with distinctly conservative politics. It's more important to their employers that they continue their advocacy than that they comply with professional guidelines or ethical requirements. The lesson of the Weinstein and Lott cases seems to be that you can get away with scholarly misconduct if you work outside the university and if the positions you are defending have powerful supporters.

For those who work inside the university, the lessons are more mixed. I have argued here that Emory University was too harsh in the Bellesiles case and too negligent with Fox-Genovese. David Abraham deserved a history job at Catholic University or Santa Cruz or Texas. But in several other cases at other schools, the proceedings seem fair: Mount Holyoke punishing but keeping Joseph Ellis, Franklin and Marshall not punishing Edward Pearson, CUNY firing Dino Cinel, and SUNY-Stony Brook hiring Mike Davis despite the attacks on his work.

The "cheating culture" thesis holds that dishonesty has become more widespread recently—not only in the corporate world but also in the world of scholarship. Most commentators on the recent round of historians in trouble argue against this view and assert that scholarly misconduct now is not more widespread than it was in the past.[13] It is simply more visible. In this view, understanding historians in trouble requires looking not at new cultural values but rather at the media. Ron Robin is the leading advocate of this interpretation. "The alleged climate of decline," he writes in *Scandals and Scoundrels,* results primarily from new "modes of visibility" and "avenues of dissemination." In the past, historians in trouble typically were granted the privilege of secluded adjudication, whereas today we see more media events around scholarly misconduct, "staged and choreographed for mass spectatorship."[14]

But Ron Robin doesn't really provide evidence that there was less intellectual fraud in the past. He offers only a single anecdote: George Kennan's 1951 inquest into the "Sisson documents," which had purported to prove the Bolshevik leaders in 1917 were paid agents of the German General Staff. J. Franklin Jameson, former

editor of the *American Historical Review,* had proclaimed the documents genuine, but Kennan showed they had been forged. Yet Kennan's evidence was "greeted with public indifference"—in contrast
to today's scholarly scandals.[15] It's a great story, and a significant
one, but it hardly proves that the scandals of yesteryear were as
frequent as today's.

At the end of this story, almost all of the historians in trouble discussed here recovered and continued their careers. Dino Cinel provides one exception: he no longer has an academic position; his
record of sexual exploitation of young people ended his career as an
academic, as it should have. But Doris Kearns Goodwin is back on
TV as a political commentator. David Abraham is a prominent professor of law. Mike Davis is a tenured history professor. Joseph Ellis
is back in the classroom and in the *New York Times Book Review.*
Stephen Ambrose died, but until his death he continued to write
bestsellers. Edward Pearson remains chair of his department. John
Lott continues his work at a private think tank. Elizabeth Fox-
Genovese and Stephan Thernstrom still serve on the board of the
National Council on the Humanities. Allen Weinstein as of this
writing is scheduled for Senate confirmation hearings as Archivist of
the United States.

That leaves Michael Bellesiles, the historian of gun culture
whose book was found to contain errors. His errors were many and
serious. He is the only one whose career was ended because of problems in his scholarship. Is that because his offenses were the most
serious of the cases reviewed here? Or because his critics outside the

university were the most powerful and the most determined? Virtually no historians at universities or colleges demanded that Emory get rid of Bellesiles, or that Vintage withdraw his book, or that Columbia withdraw his prize. If there were historians—faculty members at colleges or universities—who favored those steps, they did not say so in print.[16] David Garrow, for example, who argued in print that Joseph Ellis should be fired and "barred from ever again teaching history" anywhere, in the Bellesiles case favored only "a completely thorough investigation and report."[17] Even the Emory outside review committee that charged Bellesiles with "fraud" in his Table 1 did not recommend firing him. In fact they made no recommendation.

My conclusion is that Bellesiles suffered the most serious punishment not because his offenses were the most serious, but because his opponents were the most powerful. Thus in the end we return to the issue of power.

Some cases end up as media spectacles while others do not for the same reasons that some careers are ended while others are not— and indeed the same reason why some historians are honored with White House nominations while others are not: because of the power of organized advocacy groups outside the academy. Where power is exercised, historians are rewarded and historians are punished.

The real need over the longer term is to find ways to counter the excessive power of right-wing advocacy groups. On many issues to-day, the right adopts uncompromising tactics and a combative stance. Those who don't share their values, who are in the political center as well as on the left, often lack the single-minded zeal of activists on the right and have priorities in their lives other than fulfilling particular political agendas. Many are reluctant to speak out in an assertive voice. In the end, the power of the right turns out to be a problem not just for historians in trouble, but also for the rest of us.

Update:
The Allen Weinstein Nomination

*T*he Senate Governmental Affairs Committee held a confirmation hearing for Allen Weinstein as Archivist of the United States in July 2004. Weinstein himself was the only witness. What might have been an uneventful day was disrupted by Senator Carl Levin, Democrat from Michigan, who declared that the current archivist, John Carlin, said he been asked by the White House to resign but that the White House had not given him any reason. Levin noted that this move was apparently in violation of the 1984 law which set the term of the archivist as indefinite and declared that the president could remove the archivist only for cause and only if he gave reasons to Congress.

That switched the focus of the hearing away from Weinstein and his qualifications to Bush and his motives. "Mr. Carlin may be willing to leave at the request of the White House," Levin said, "but we have an obligation to protect the objectivity of the Archives and to find out why the White House asked him to leave."

Senator Joseph Lieberman, Democrat of Connecticut, took up the argument, telling Weinstein "you're coming in . . . to carry out a more secretive policy at the Archives, perhaps even to protect records of this administration or the previous Bush administration," which under the law would be subject to release in January 2005. Lieberman also criticized Weinstein for declaring in his answers to written questions that, as archivist, he would defend in court the Bush executive order on classification, which significantly reduces access to presidential papers.

Republican Susan Collins of Maine, committee chair, told Weinstein that "there has been concern expressed by some scholars who say that you failed to make available for review by other scholars the notes and records that you relied upon" in writing *Perjury* and *The Haunted Wood*. He had told the committee staff that he planned to donate the materials in question to the Hoover Institution. She then asked him point-blank, "Do you plan to impose restrictions that would limit public access to those notes once they're donated?" Weinstein answered, "No. . . . they'll be all available."

Because Levin and Lieberman made it clear that they would not support a new archivist unless the White House came up with adequate cause for removing the current one, "the Weinstein nomination may well be in deep trouble," according to Bruce Craig of the National Coalition for History—especially if George W. Bush is not reelected.[1]

For additional updates, see www.JonWiener.com

Notes

Introduction: Historians in Trouble

1. See Ira Berlin, "Trust," *OAH Newsletter* 31:1 (February 2003), www.oah.org/pubs/nl/2003feb/berlin.html (accessed March 6, 2004).
2. Ron Robin, *Scandals and Scoundrels: Seven Cases That Shook the Academy* (Berkeley: University of California Press, 2004), 9–10. The concept of the "media spectacle" comes from Guy Debord, *Society of the Spectacle* (Detroit: Black and Red, 1967). For a recent work developing the concept, see Douglas Kellner, *Media Spectacle* (New York: Routledge, 2003).
3. E.H. Carr, *What Is History?* (New York: Vintage Books, 1967), 8.
4. Thomas Mallon, *Stolen Words* (New York: Harcourt, 1989; Penguin, 1991).

1. Feminism and Harassment: Elizabeth Fox-Genovese Goes to Court

1. Jacqueline Trescott, "Medalists Span Arts Spectrum," *Washington Post,* November 13, 2003, C4; "President Bush Awards 2003 Humanities Medals," www.neh.gov/news/archive/20031114.html (accessed March 6, 2004). Fox-Genovese was already a member of the National Council on the Humanities.
2. Mark Silk, "Emory Settles Sex Bias Case: Renowned Historian Accused of Harassment, Discrimination," *Atlanta Journal-Constitution,* March 22, 1996, 1D. The White House also did not note that Fox-Genovese had been an editor of the journal *Marxist Perspectives* during its brief life from 1978 to 1980. The masthead in the first issue listed her as "International Affairs" editor, with her husband Eugene D. Genovese as editor. (I was also listed on the masthead as "Organizational Secretary" for Irvine.) The second issue included her article, "Yves Saint Laurent's Peasant Revolution," *Marxist Perspectives* 1:2

(Summer 1978), 58–93. After the fall of the Soviet Union, the two Genoveses abandoned Marxism and in 1995 embraced the Catholic Church—she converted. They posed for a photograph for the *Atlanta Journal-Constitution* kneeling in prayer at the Cathedral of Christ the King. The photo was captioned, "Now a Eucharistic minister at Christ the King, Betsey Fox-Genovese says that the day in 1995 when she made her confession, received Communion for the first time, was confirmed and remarried her husband in a religious ceremony 'wove together the essential threads of the preceding 53 years of my life.'" Michael Skube, "A Change of Heart: He was a Committed Communist; They Were Both Nonbelievers. Then Scholars Eugene and Elizabeth Fox-Genovese Found God and Grace in the Roman Catholic Church," *Atlanta Journal-Constitution*, August 1, 1999, 1M.

3. Ibid.

4. For the charges, see First Amended Complaint, *Virginia Gould v. Emory University and Elizabeth Fox-Genovese,* civil action file no. 93-1469-3, Superior Court of DeKalb County, State of Georgia, box 6549, fiche 12 [subsequent citations to *"Gould v. Emory"*]; Lolita Browning, "Harassment Case Goes to Trial," *Fulton County (GA) Daily Report,* March 15, 1996; Mark Silk, "Court Notes: Jury, Publicity Caused Agreement; Fox-Genovese Trial Threatened All Parties," *Atlanta Journal-Constitution,* March 28, 1996, 15A; Mark Silk, "Trial of the Professor and Her Ex-Protégé Begins After 3 Years," *Atlanta Journal-Constitution,* March 18, 1996, 1B.

5. Mark Silk, "Emory Settles Sex Bias Case," *Atlanta Journal-Constitution,* March 22, 1996.

6. For a list of those deposed, see *Gould v. Emory,* box 6551, fiche 1 and 2, and box 6552, fiche 1.

7. Dr. Robert W. Ethridge, Assistant Vice President, memo to Dean Eleanor Main, the Graduate School, October 11, 1991; Exhibit "F," *Gould v. Emory,* box 6548, fiche 12. Ethridge memo quoted in Silk, "Trial of the Professor." Ethridge today is vice president of equal opportunity programs at Emory. The *Emory Report* recently declared that the school's administration had "no one . . . more even-tempered, more approachable" than he, and explained that "his job is to diffuse trouble, and—whenever he can—prevent it." Eric Rangus, "The Manner of the Man," *Emory Report,* January 13, 2003, www.emory.edu/EMORY_REPORT/erarchive/2003/January/erJan.13/1_13_03profile.html (accessed March 6, 2004).

8. Patricia McGarry, "Document Product" (notarized statement), *Gould v. Emory,* box 6548, fiche 15.

9. "Affidavit of Lisa Tyree," Exhibit "H," *Gould v. Emory,* box 6548, fiche 18.

10. Sarah Elbert quoted in "Proceedings" (Opening Arguments, May 24, 1995), *Gould v. Emory,* box 6550, fiche 10, 87.

11. "Plaintiff's Supplemental Response to Emory University's Second Interrogatories," *Gould v. Emory,* box 6548, fiche 3, 2–3. Stephanie McCurry, *Masters of Small Worlds: Yeoman Households, Gender Relations, and the Political Culture of the Antebellum South Carolina Low Country* (New York: Oxford University Press, 1995). The book won the 1995 John Hope Franklin Prize of the American Studies Association as the outstanding book published in American studies, and the 1995 Charles S. Sydnor Award of the Southern Historical Association for the outstanding book published in southern history.

12. "Affidavit of Dr. Pat Michelson," *Gould v. Emory,* box 6548, fiche 21.

13. "Plaintiff's Supplemental Response," *Gould v. Emory,* 6–7.

14. Ibid., 8–9.

15. Ibid., 10.

16. Ibid., 2.

17. Ibid., 13.

18. Laura Clark Brown, Head of Public Services, University of North Carolina Libraries Manuscript Department, to Jon Wiener, September 24, 2003 (in author's possession). The Fox-Genovese collection is described at the archives website, www.lib.unc.edu/mss/inv/htm/04851.html (accessed March 6, 2004).

19. Elizabeth Fox-Genovese, *Feminism Without Illusions: A Critique of Individualism* (Chapel Hill: University of North Carolina Press, 1991). Afterword quoted in "Defendant Fox-Genovese's Motion in Limine to Exclude the Dog Training Metaphor in Fox-Genovese's Book," *Gould v. Emory,* box 6548, fiche 4.

20. "Defendant Fox-Genovese's Motion," ibid.

21. "Reply Brief in Support of Defendant's and Emory University's Motion for Summary Judgment," *Gould v. Emory,* box 6548, fiche 1, 9–10.

22. "First Amended Complaint," *Gould v. Emory,* box 6549, fiche 12, 5–6.

23. "Proceedings," *Gould v. Emory,* box 6550, fiche 10, 28.

24. Ibid., 55.

25. Ibid., 78.

26. Ibid., 85–86. Claire Guthrie Gastañaga has an interesting website at www.preventivepractices.com/Claire_Guthrie_Gastanaga.html (accessed March 6, 2004).

27. Elbert quoted in "Proceedings," *Gould v. Emory,* 87.

28. Ibid., 88.

29. Robin Wilson, "Prize-Winning Author Arrested on Charges of Harassing University Employee," *Chronicle of Higher Education,* October 18, 2002, 14.

30. Mae Gentry, "Emory Prof Sits Out Semester; King Biographer Accused of Abuse Last Year," *Atlanta Journal-Constitution,* August 28, 2003, 10C.

31. "Law and Order," *Atlanta Journal-Constitution,* September 19, 2003, 7C.

32. Mae Gentry, "Emory Suspends King Biographer Following Arrest," *Atlanta Journal-Constitution,* October 23, 2002, 1B.

33. Ibid.; see also "Nation in Brief," *Washington Post,* October 24, 2002, A36.

34. Mary Zeiss Stange, "The Political Intolerance of Academic Feminism," *Chronicle of Higher Education,* June 21, 2002, 16.

35. Richard Morgan, "Judging Public Intellectuals," *Chronicle of Higher Education,* January 18, 2002, 6.

36. Cynthia Grenier, "Skewering Left's Take on History," *Washington Times,* June 15, 2002, B1.

37. Susan Faludi, review of *Feminism Is Not the Story of My Life,* by Elizabeth Fox-Genovese, *The Nation,* January 8, 1996, 25. See also Elinor Burkett, *The Right Women: A Journal Through the Heart of Conservative America* (New York: Scribner, 1998), 207–11.

38. Mary Gordon, "What Makes a Woman a Woman," review of *Feminism Is Not the Story of My Life,* by Fox-Genovese, *New York Times Book Review,* January 14, 1996, 9.

39. Ruth Conniff, review of *Feminism Is Not the Story of My Life,* by Fox-Genovese, *Progressive,* January 1997, 33.

40. Elizabeth Kristol, "The Sexual Devolution," review of *Feminism Is Not the Story of My Life,* by Fox-Genovese, *Commentary,* April 1996, 59; "The Un-Feminist," *Washington Times,* April 25, 1996, A2; Claudia Winkler, "Story of Their Lives," review of *Feminism Is Not the Story of My Life,* by Fox-Genovese, *Weekly Standard,* January 22, 1996, 34.

41. "Unpublished Letters, Brites, and More," *Weekly Standard,* November 24, 2003.

2. The Alger Hiss Case, the Archives, and Allen Weinstein

1. "What Is the National Archives & Records Administration?" http://www. archives.gov/about_us/what_is_nara/what_is_nara.html (accessed May 12, 2004). Portions of this chapter originally published as "The Archives and Allen Weinstein," *The Nation,* May 17, 2004, 17–19, "The Alger Hiss Case, the Archives, and Allen Weinstein," *Perspectives: Newsmagazine of the American Historical Association* 30 (February 1992), 10–12; "Compromised Positions," *Lingua Franca,* January–February 1993, 41–48; "Historian with a History," *Los Angeles Times,* May 2, 2004, M1.

2. Society of American Archivists, "Statement on the Nomination of Allen Weinstein to Become Archivist of the United States," www.archivists.org/ statements/weinstein.asp (accessed April 27, 2004). See also Sheryl Gay Stolberg and Felicia R. Lee, "Bush Nominee for Archivist Is Criticized for His Secrecy," *New York Times,* April 20, 2004, A14; Stewart M. Powell, "Archivist Shake-Up Raises Document-Release Concerns," *Houston Chronicle,* April 25, 2004, A7.

3. Bruce Craig, "The Weinstein Nomination—An Update," *National Coalition for History Washington Update* 10, April 23, 2004, http://h-net.msu.edu/cgibin/ logbrowse.pl?trx=vx&list=H-NCH&month=0404&week=d&msg=7UhaKiM m/gmZYfN5YKVWdQ&user=&pw= (accessed April 27, 2004).

4. Society of American Archivists, "A Code of Ethics for Archivists," www. archivists.org/governance/handbook/app_ethics.asp (accessed April 27, 2004).

5. Quoted in Esther B. Fein, "Book Notes: Gold in Archives," *New York Times,* July 29, 1992, C20.

6. Joyce Appleby, e-mail to author, April 23, 2004; Ellen Schrecker, "The Spies Who Loved Us?" *The Nation,* May 24, 1999, 28.

7. Amy Knight, "The Selling of the KGB: Media Accounts KGB Espionage," *Wilson Quarterly* 24:1 (January 1, 2000), 16.

8. Anna Kasten Nelson, "Illuminating the Twilight Struggle: New Interpretations of the Cold War," *Chronicle of Higher Education,* June 25, 1999, B4. On Nelson's qualifications, see "Testimony of Anna K. Nelson: Subcommittee on Government Efficiency, Financial Management and Intergovernmental Relations, Committee on Government Reform, November 6, 2001," concerning the release of presidential papers, www.fas.org/sgp/congress/2001/110601_ anelson.html (accessed March 22, 2004).

9. Susan Butler, letter to *The Nation,* October 15, 2001.

10. Sam Tanenhaus, "Tangled Treason," *New Republic,* July 5, 1999, 28.

11. Allen Weinstein, *Perjury: The Hiss-Chambers Case* (New York: Knopf, 1978); Victor Navasky, "Allen Weinstein's 'Perjury': The Case Not Proved Against Alger Hiss," *The Nation,* April 8, 1978, 393–401.

12. Victor Navasky, letter to the editor, *New Republic,* May 13, 1978, 38.

13. "Allen Weinstein Replies," *New Republic,* May 13, 1978, 38. He made the same pledge elsewhere: "the files on which I based my research . . . will be deposited in the Truman Library." Weinstein quoted in David Farrell, "Hiss Case Chronicler Lashes Back," *Boston Globe,* April 23, 1978.

14. "Statement on Standards of Professional Conduct," *Perspectives: Newsmagazine of the American Historical Association,* March 1989, 16–18.

15. "Statement on Interviewing for Historical Documentation," *Perspectives: Newsmagazine of the American Historical Association,* October 1989, 8.

16. Allen Weinstein, "The Alger Hiss Case Revisited," *American Scholar* 41 (1971–72), 121.

17. "Key Hiss-Chambers Site is Given Landmark Status," *New York Times,* May 18, 1988.

18. "Hiss: A New Book Finds Him Guilty as Charged," *Time,* February 13, 1978, 28–30; Garry Wills, review of *Perjury,* by Allen Weinstein, *New York Review of Books,* April 20, 1978, 29; T.S. Matthews, review of *Perjury,* by Weinstein, *New Republic,* April 8, 1978, 27; Allen Weinstein, " 'Perjury,' Take Three," *New Republic,* May 13, 1978, 16–21.

19. George F. Will, "The Myth of Alger Hiss," *Newsweek,* March 20, 1978, 96.

20. Alfred Kazin, "Why Hiss Can't Confess," *Esquire,* March 28, 1978, 21–22. For another favorable review, see Irving Howe, review of *Perjury,* by Weinstein, *New York Times Book Review,* April 9, 1978, 1. In the *American Historical Review,* the book was reviewed by Ronald Radosh, who would publish a similar book five years later arguing that Julius and Ethel Rosenberg were guilty of espionage. Ronald Radosh, review of *Perjury,* by Weinstein, *American Historical Review* 84 (1979), 586; see also Richard Kirkendall, review of *Perjury,* by Weinstein, *Journal of American History* 66 (1979), 206.

21. Weinstein, *Perjury,* 114, 124.

22. Navasky, "Allen Weinstein's 'Perjury,' " *The Nation,* April 8, 1978, 396, 398.

23. Weinstein, *Perjury,* 62, 129.

24. Navasky, "Allen Weinstein's 'Perjury,' " 397.

25. Weinstein, *Perjury,* 313–14n.

26. Navasky, "Allen Weinstein's 'Perjury,' " 399.

27. Weinstein, *Perjury,* 100n.

28. Navasky, "Allen Weinstein's 'Perjury,' " 401.

29. Garry Wills, telephone interview with author, December 1991. See especially Garry Wills, afterword to "Alger Hiss" (reprint of a *New York Review* essay) in Wills, *Lead Time: A Journalist's Education* (New York, 1983), 61–62.

30. "Weinstein's Controversial Hiss-Chambers Probe Now Scheduled for April Release by Knopf," *Publishers Weekly,* December 12, 1977, 43.

31. "Allen Weinstein Replies," *New Republic,* May 13, 1978, 38.

32. Victor Navasky, "Waiting for Weinstein," *The Nation,* April 22, 1978, 451.

33. Michael Kernan, "A Literary Skirmish Over Hiss," *Washington Post,* April 6, 1978, B3.

34. Navasky, letter to the editor, *New Republic,* 38.

35. "Allen Weinstein Replies," 38.

36. Warren Hinckle, "The Hiss/Weinstein File," *The Nation,* June 17, 1978, 718–19.

37. Weinstein, " 'Perjury,' Take Three," 19.

38. "Allen Weinstein Statement," *New Republic,* June 7 & 14, 1979, 11.

39. "Costly Error for Hiss Historian," *New York,* May 21, 1979, 61. Another source gave the figure as $17,500: "Krieger Victorious over Hiss Author," *Village Voice,* May 28, 1979, 31; Krieger wrote that he "settled for a sum that barely covered legal costs": Sam Krieger, "An Historian's Falsehoods," *Rights* (published by the National Emergency Civil Liberties Committee), September–October 1979, 12.

40. Christoper Lehmann-Haupt, review of *Perjury,* by Weinstein, *New York Times,* April 7, 1978, section III, 25.

41. William Reuben, telephone interview with author, December 1991; see Reuben, "Hiss Perjury Trials," *Encyclopedia of the American Left,* Mari Jo Buhle, Paul Buhle, Dan Georgakas, eds. (New York: Garland, 1990), 314–17.

42. Ronald Grele, telephone interview with author, December 1991.

43. Dennis Bilger, telephone interview with author, December 1991.

44. Dennis Bilger, e-mail to Eileen Luhr, June 11, 2003, in author's possession.

45. Garry Wills quoted in "The Hiss Case, Cont'd," *Newsweek,* April 17, 1978, 92.

46. Garry Wills, telephone interview with author, December 1991.

47. Allen Weinstein, *Perjury: The Hiss-Chambers Case* (New York: Random House, 1997), "Note on Documentation."

48. Victor Navasky, "Allen Weinstein's Docudrama," review of *Perjury: The Hiss-Chambers Case* (1997 edition), by Weinstein, *The Nation,* November 3, 1997,

11, www.thenation.com/doc.mhtml?i=19971103&s-navasky (accessed March 26, 2004).

49. Press release for the new edition of *Perjury,* quoted in ibid.

50. Allen Weinstein posted his bio at www.centerfordemocracy.org/awbio.html (accessed March 17, 2004).

51. Allen Weinstein, "The Enemy Within," *Washington Post,* January 20, 2002, T03; Weinstein, "Thinner than Water," *Los Angeles Times Book Review,* November 11, 2001, 4.

52. For example: David Evanier, "Invincible Ignorance," *Weekly Standard,* November 17, 2003: "The revisionists have replicated this sealed, Alice-in-Wonderland world in the ivory towers of academia, far from the sweaty realities of the streets and their beloved masses. Incredibly enough, it is a domain they largely control, imposing their fantasies on students, leading historical journals and textbooks, and on the entire history profession." Also: Gov. Frank Keating, "Shades of Pink," *National Review,* May 19, 2001: "All three of our children seem to have survived their travels through the left-wing fever swamps of academia, and for that we are grateful. . . . I was unaware of how extreme the left-wing fringes of academia had become—and how dominant some of these crackpots have become on many campuses—until I scanned the course offerings listed by some of our most 'elite' schools."

3. Facing Black Students at Harvard: Stephan Thernstrom Takes a Stand

1. William B. Higgins, "President Nominates Harvard Professor," *Harvard Crimson,* January 22, 2003, www.thecrimson.com/article.aspx?ref=261887 (accessed March 7, 2004). Portions of this chapter were originally published as "What Happened at Harvard," *The Nation,* September 30, 1991, 384–88.

2. Stephan Thernstrom and Abigail Thernstrom, *America in Black and White: Race in Modern America* (New York: Simon & Schuster, 1997); Abigail Thernstrom and Stephan Thernstrom, *No Excuses: Closing the Racial Gap in Learning America* (New York: Simon & Schuster, 2003); see also Peter Schrag, "How the Other Half Learns," review of *No Excuses,* by Thernstrom and Thernstrom, *The Nation,* November 10, 2003, 23–24. The definitive piece is Adam Shatz, "The Thernstroms in Black and White," *American Prospect* 12:5 (March 12, 2001), www.prospect.org/print/V12/5/shatz-a.html (accessed February 28, 2004).

3. Eugene D. Genovese, "Heresy, Yes—Sensitivity, No," review of *Illiberal Education: The Politics of Race and Sex on Campus,* by Dinesh D'Souza, *New Republic,* April 15, 1991, 30; C. Vann Woodward, "Freedom and the Universities," review of *Illiberal Education,* by D'Souza, *New York Review of Books,* July 18, 1991, 32.

4. Dinesh D'Souza, *Illiberal Education: The Politics of Race and Sex on Campus* (New York: Free Press, 1991), 196–97.

5. Letter from Stephan Thernstrom to the *Harvard Crimson,* February 9, 1988, as quoted in D'Souza, *Illiberal Education,* 195.

6. Orlando Patterson, telephone interview with author, September 1991.

7. Paula Ford, telephone interview with author, September 1991.

8. Wendi Grantham, telephone interview with author, September 1991.

9. Wendi Grantham, "Course Displayed Racial Insensitivity," *Harvard Crimson,* February 17, 1988, www.thecrimson.com/article.aspx?ref=132930 (accessed February 28, 2004).

10. D'Souza, *Illiberal Education,* 196.

11. Ibid.

12. Ibid.

13. Fred Jewett, telephone interview with author, September 1991.

14. A. Michael Spence, "AMS Statement 3/8/88," 3, in author's possession. Thanks to Associate Dean Phyllis Keller for faxing this document.

15. D'Souza, *Illiberal Education,* 197. Genovese agreed, writing that the Harvard administration in the Thernstrom case was "doing their best to create an atmosphere in which professors who value their reputations . . . learn to censor themselves." Genovese, "Heresy," 30.

16. John Taylor, "Are You Politically Correct?" *New York,* January 21, 1991, 32.

17. Stephan Thernstrom, telephone interview with author, September 1991.

18. D'Souza, *Illiberal Education,* 195.

19. Hilda Hernandez-Gravelle, telephone interview with author, September 1991.

20. John Womack, telephone interview with author, September 1991.

21. Martin Kilson, telephone interview with author, September 1991.

22. The *Crimson* articles are all available on-line. For coverage of Dean Spence's defense of Thernstrom, see Susan B. Glasser, "Dean Comments on Complaint," *Harvard Crimson,* March 10, 1988, www.thecrimson.com/article.aspx?ref=270906; for students' defense of Thernstrom, see Jesper B. Sorenson, "A Common Academic Ground," *Harvard Crimson,* March 8, 1988, www.thecrimson.com/article.aspx?ref=158535 and Emily Mieras, "Thernstrom

Only Provoking Original Thoughts," *Harvard Crimson,* February 17, 1988, www.thecrimson.com/article.aspx?ref=132931; for an example of Thernstrom defending himself, see Susan B. Glasser, "Thernstrom Waits for Charges: After Charges of Racial Insensitivity, Professor Hears Nothing," *Harvard Crimson,* March 5, 1988, www.thecrimson.com/article.aspx?ref=345397; for a retrospective on the case, see Susan B. Glasser, "Sensitive Issues: A Classroom Dilemma: Teaching Non-Traditional Subjects," *Harvard Crimson,* April 9, 1988, www.thecrimson.com/article.aspx?ref=242622; that article concludes, "Three students in February brought a complaint about Winthrop Professor of History Stephan A. Thernstrom to the Committee on Race Relations, a non-disciplinary, advisory body of the College. In response, Spence read his brief statement on academic freedom to the full Faculty at its March meeting. The students then met with Thernstrom and gave him a written statement of their complaints." (All accessed February 28, 2004.)

23. Higgins, "President Nominates Harvard Professor."

4. *Arming America* and "Academic Fraud"

1. The key *Times* article was Robert F. Worth, "Historian's Prizewinning Book on Guns Is Embroiled in a Scandal," *New York Times,* December 8, 2001, A13. The term "academic fraud" comes from Donald Hickey, a history professor at Wayne State College in Nebraska, quoted in Ron Grossman, "Wormy Apples from the Groves of Academe," *Chicago Tribune,* January 23, 2002, C1. Portions of this chapter were published originally as "Fire at Will: How the Critics Shot up Michael Bellesiles's *Arming America," The Nation,* November 4, 2002, 28–32; and "Emory's Bellesiles Report: A Case of Tunnel Vision," *OAH Newsletter,* February 2003, 8–9. Copyright © Organization of American Historians. Reprinted with permission.

2. Joanne Meyerowitz, "History's Ethical Crisis: An Introduction," *Journal of American History* 90:4 (March 2004), www.historycooperative.org/journals/jah/90.4/meyerowitz.html (accessed March 8, 2004).

3. Gloria L. Main, "Many Things Forgotten: The Use of Probate Records in *Arming America," William and Mary Quarterly* 59:1 (January 2002), 216.

4. Ira Gruber, "Of Arms and Men: *Arming America* and Military History," *William and Mary Quarterly* 59:1 (January 2002), 220.

5. Randolph Roth, "Guns, Gun Culture, and Homicide," *William and Mary Quarterly* 59:1 (January 2002), 223–40.

6. Two historians told me they had declined an offer of $10,000, but asked that their names remain confidential.

7. Emory posted the report at www.emory.edu/central/NEWS/Releases/Final_Report.pdf (accessed February 7, 2004), hereafter cited as "Report."

8. Report, 15, 11, 18. The committee highlighted what they termed "the implausibility of some of his defenses—a prime example is that of the 'hacking' of his website." Report, 19. A different anti-gun website was definitely a target of hacking: see www.askjohnlott.org/news.html (accessed February 7, 2004). Of course that doesn't prove that something similar happened to Bellesiles, but the parallels are interesting.

9. Laurel Thatcher Ulrich, e-mail to author, October 26, 2002.

10. Jan Gleason, assistant vice president of public affairs at Emory, telephone interview with author, October 1, 2002, referred to the Emory policy posted at www.or.emory.edu/share/policies/misconduct.html (accessed March 6, 2004)—see "Procedures," section B.11.9, for possible sanctions.

11. "Statement of Michael Bellesiles on Emory University's Inquiry into *Arming America*," "Excluded Years" section, www.emory.edu/central/NEWS/Releases/B_statement.pdf (accessed March 17, 2004).

12. Michael Bellesiles, *Arming America*, 2nd ed. (New York: Soft Skull Press, 2003) note to 445.

13. Michael Zuckerman, interview with author, October 2002.

14. In the mid-eighties, Bellesiles was a student in a couple of courses I taught at UC Irvine, where he got his Ph.D., but I had not talked to him for almost twenty years before his return to UCI in 2001.

15. Kimberly Strassel, "Academic Accountability," *Wall Street Journal*, June 6, 2002, www.opinionjournal.com/columnists/kstrassel/?id=110001806; Melissa Seckora, "Disarming America," *National Review*, October 15, 2001, www.nationalreview.com/15oct01/seckoraprint101501.html; Seckora, "Disarming America, Part II," December 6, 2001, www.nationalreview.com/nr_comment/nr_commentprint112601.html; Seckora, "Disarming America, Part III," January 29, 2002, www.nationalreview.com/nr_comment/nr_comment012902.shtml; Harvey Klehr and James Earl Haynes, "Radical History," *New Criterion* 20 (June 2002), www.newcriterion.com/archive/20/jun02/ buhle.htm; David Skinner, "The Cowards of Academe," *Weekly Standard*, June 10, 2002,

www.weeklystandard.com/content/public/articles/000/000/001/323pkmbz.asp (all accessed March 6, 2004).

16. Jacqueline Trescott, "Book Flap Prompts NEH to Pull Name from Fellowship," *Washington Post,* May 22, 2002, C3.

17. Garry Wills, "Spiking the Gun Myth," review of *Arming America,* by Michael Bellesiles, *New York Times Book Review,* September 10, 2000, 5.

18. Edmund S. Morgan, "In Love with Guns," review of *Arming America,* by Bellesiles, *New York Review of Books,* October 19, 2000, 30–32.

19. On December 21, 2000, shortly after *Arming America* was published, Bellesiles posted on the H-OIEAHC discussion board at H-NET a proposal to "create a web site devoted to probate records." In that posting he declared, "My own material is in a sorry state because of the great Bowden Hall Flood of 2000 (the pipes in Emory's History building burst this summer). My original note pads have all been dried out, though many pages are a ruined pulp." http://h-net. msu.edu/cgi-bin/logbrowse.pl?trx=vx&list=h-oieahc&month=0012&week=d& msg=eUkFWuw4/iZoyynC2YXMNA&user=&pw= (accessed February 7, 2004).

20. James Lindgren and Justin Lee Heather, "Counting Guns in Early America," *William and Mary Law Review* 42:5 (2002), www.law.nwu.edu/faculty/ fulltime/Lindgren/Lindgren.html (accessed March 17, 2004). Lindgren is cited, among other places, in Kimberly A. Strassel, "Academic Accountability," *Wall Street Journal,* June 6, 2002, www.opinionjournal.com/columnists/kstrassel/?id= 110001806 (accessed March 19, 2004).

21. Jack Rakove, "Words, Deeds, and Guns: *Arming America* and the Second Amendment," *William and Mary Quarterly* 59:1 (January 2002), 209, www.historycooperative.org/journals/wm/59.1.rakove.html (accessed March 19, 2004).

22. Michael Bellesiles, *Arming America: The Origins of a National Gun Culture* (New York: Knopf, 2000), 173.

23. Alexander Cockburn, "Beat the Devil: The Year of the Yellow Notepad," *The Nation,* April 8, 2002, 8.

24. Originally Bellesiles posted his "San Francisco" probate records at www. emory.edu/history/bellesiles/sfprobate.html; they can be found now at www. bellesiles.com (accessed March 31, 2004).

25. Betty Maffei, "Notes on Supposed San Francisco Records in the Contra Costa County Historical Society History Center," *Arms Rights and Liberty,* www.rkba.org/research/bellesiles/ccchs-sf.html (accessed March 29, 2004).

26. Ron Grossman, "Wormy Apples."

27. *Arming America*, first edition, 386.

28. The "San Francisco" probate records are not included in table 1 in the second edition of the book.

29. Randolph Roth, "Guns, Gun Culture, and Homicide: The Relationship between Firearms, the Uses of Firearms, and Interpersonal Violence," *William and Mary Quarterly* 59:1 (January 2002), 223, 40, www.historycooperative. org/journals/wm/59.1/roth.html (accessed March 18, 2004).

30. James Lindgren, "Fall from Grace: *Arming America* and the Bellesiles Scandal," *Yale Law Review* 111:8 (June 2002), www.law.northwestern.edu/ faculty/fulltime/Lindgren/LindgrenFINAL.pdf, 2232 (accessed March 6, 2004).

31. Mary Beth Norton, telephone interview with author, October 2002.

32. Danny Postel, "Did the Shootouts over 'Arming America' Divert Attention from the Real Issues?" *Chronicle of Higher Education*, February 1, 2002, www.viewandreviews/com/free/v48/i21/21a01201.htm (accessed March 17, 2004).

33. James Lindgren, e-mail to author headed "OFF THE RECORD, CONFIDENTIAL," September 2, 2002.

34. Postel, "Did the Shootouts?"

35. Matthew Warshauer, telephone interview with author, October 2002.

36. Neil Vidmar and Michael J. Saks, "A Flawed Search for Bias in the American Bar Association's Ratings of Judicial Nominees: A Critique of the Lindgren/Federalist Society Study," *Journal of Law & Politics* 17:2 (2001), http://papers.ssrn.com/abstract=293783 (accessed March 17, 2004).

37. See Lindgren's list of publications at www.law.nwu.edu/faculty/fulltime/ Lindgren/Lindgren.html (accessed March 17, 2004). Lindgren also did some work on the pro-gun research fraud of John Lott, but didn't publish it, give lectures about it, or write reviewers of Lott's book—see below, chapter 8, note 28.

38. Michael Bellesiles, telephone interview with author, October 2002; *WMQ* editor Christopher Grasso said in a telephone interview with the author (October 2002) that it was standard policy of the journal to correct errors before publication whenever possible.

39. http:/talk.shooters.com/room_7/feb262002.cfm (accessed March 1, 2002).

40. www.keepandbeararms.com/information/XcIBViewItem.asp?ID=2376 (accessed March 17, 2004).

41. Angel Shamaya, e-mail to Matthew Warshauer, August 19, 2002, in author's possession.

42. See Gary B. Nash, Charlotte Crabtree, Ross E. Dunn, *History on Trial: Culture Wars and the Teaching of the Past* (New York: Knopf, 1998); Todd Gitlin, *The Twilight of Common Dreams: Why America Is Wracked by Culture Wars* (New York: Henry Holt, 1995).

43. Ronald Radosh, "The Triumph of Ideological History," www.front pagemagazine.com/Articles/ReadArticle.asp?ID=1474, February 1, 2002 (accessed May 11, 2004); Harvey Klehr and John Earl Haynes, "Radical History," *New Criterion* 20:10 (June 2002), www.newcriterion.com/archive/20/jun02/buhle.htm (accessed March 17, 2004). The *National Review* website lists twenty articles on Bellesiles, led by Melissa Seckora, "Disarming America," *National Review Online,* October 15, 2001; "Disarming America, Part II," December 6, 2001; "Disarming America, Part III," January 29, 2002; www.nationalreview.com (accessed April 2, 2002). Charlton Heston, letter to the editor, *New York Times Book Review,* October 1, 2000, 4. Heston quoted in Tim Cornwell, "Who Said Your Daddy's Daddy Won the West with the Help of a Gun?" *Times Higher Education Supplement,* November 10, 2000, 20.

44. Jerome Sternstein, "'Pulped' Fiction: Michael Bellesiles and his Yellow Note Pads," http://historynewsnetwork.org/articles/article.html?id=742 (accessed March 17, 2004).

45. Cramer, "Shot in the Dark," www.nationalreview.com/weekend/books/books cramer092300.shtml; Shotgun News at www.claytoncramer.com/popular magazines.htm; money solicitation on initial page at www.claytoncramer.com (all accessed March 17, 2004).

46. Quoted in Postel, "Did the Shootouts?"

47. For the AHA and OAH statements, see *OAH Newsletter,* November 2001, www.oah.org/pubs/nl/2001nov/bellesiles.html (accessed March 17, 2004).

48. Michael Bellesiles, "Exploring America's Gun Culture," *William and Mary Quarterly* 59:1 (January 2002), www.historycooperative.org/journals/wm/59.1/bellesiles.html; Bellesiles, "Disarming the Critics," *OAH Newsletter,* November 2001, www.oah.org/pubs/nl/2001nov/Bellesiles.html (both accessed March 17, 2004).

49. David Mehegan, "Prize-winning Historian's Book Research under Scrutiny," *Boston Globe,* August 21, 2002, C2. Other newspapers that ran similar stories include: *Chattanooga Times,* August 26, 2002; *Manchester Union Leader,* August 26, 2002; *Arkansas Democrat-Gazette,* August 24, 2002; *Augusta Chronicle,*

August 24, 2002; *Deseret News,* August 24, 2002; *Milwaukee Journal,* August 24, 2002; *St. Louis Post-Dispatch,* August 24, 2002; *Atlanta Journal-Constitution,* August 24, 2002; *Washington Times,* August 23, 2002.

50. The editors at Vintage Books, which had published the first paperback edition, stuck with Bellesiles until the end but decided against publishing the revised edition "for marketing reasons." Jane Garrett, e-mail to author, September 27, 2002. The second edition was published by Soft Skull Press of Brooklyn in September 2003. Bellesiles was criticized for not publishing his second edition with a university press, which would have involved peer review. David Glenn, "Small Press Republishes Controversial Book on America's Gun Culture," *Chronicle of Higher Education,* January 9, 2004; I agree with that view.

51. Bellesiles, Introduction to *Arming America,* second edition, 1–16.

52. Mary Beth Norton, telephone interview with author, October 2002.

53. Michael Zuckerman, telephone interview with author, October 2002.

54. The Kammen quote appears as a blurb for the book; Michael Kammen, e-mail to author, September 3, 2002. On Morgan and Wills, see Postel, "Did the Shootouts?"; Garry Wills, telephone interview with author, October 2002. The second edition of *Arming America* features blurbs from Kammen and Zuckerman and a quote from Morgan's review. For the Wills quote, see the Soft Skull Press website, www.softskull.com/dtailedbook.php?isbn=1-932360-0707 (accessed August 6, 2004).

5. David Abraham and the Nazis

1. Portions of this chapter originally published as "Footnotes to History," *The Nation,* February 16, 1985, 180–83. For another discussion of the case, see Peter Novick, *That Noble Dream: The 'Objectivity Question' and the American Historical Profession* (New York: Cambridge University Press, 1988), 612–21. See also "12 Comments on the David Abraham Case," *Radical History Review* 32 (March 1985), 75–96.

2. Lawrence Stone, telephone interview with author, January 1985; Natalie Davis, telephone interview with author, January 1985.

3. Carl Schorske, telephone interview with author, January 1985.

4. Stone, interview with author.

5. On Namier and Le Roy Ladurrie: ibid.

6. Ibid.

7. Colin Campbell, "History and Ethics: A Dispute," *New York Times,* December 23, 1984, 19.

8. Arno Mayer, "A Letter to Henry Turner," *Radical History Review* 32 (March 1985), 85–86.

9. Henry Turner, letter in *American Historical Review* 88 (October 1983), 1148–49.

10. Timothy Tackett, telephone interview with author, January 1985.

11. The Nocken essay was eventually published in a toned-down version, followed by a reply from Abraham: see Novick, *That Noble Dream,* 615n55.

12. Gerald Feldman, telephone interview with author, January 1985.

13. Feldman letters, quoted in Novick, *That Noble Dream,* 614–15.

14. Feldman, interview with author. More than a decade later, Hanna Gray served on Emory's external review committee on Michael Bellesiles.

15. Stanley Katz, telephone interview with author, January 1985. More than a decade later, Katz served on Emory's external review committee on Michael Bellesiles.

16. Gerald Feldman, "A Collapse in Weimar Scholarship," *Central European History* 17 (1984), 159, 161.

17. David Abraham, "A Reply to Gerald Feldman," *Central European History* 17 (1984), 183–84.

18. Gerald Feldman, "A Response to David Abraham's Reply," *Central European History* 17 (1984), 266, 252.

19. David Abraham, *Collapse of the Weimar Republic Political Economy and Crisis* (Princeton: Princeton University Press, 1981), dedication.

20. James Joll, "Business as Usual," *New York Review of Books* 32:14 (September 26, 1985).

21. Henry Ashby Turner, *German Big Business and the Rise of Hitler* (New York: Oxford University Press, 1985), 356.

22. Abraham, *Collapse of the Weimar Republic,* 285.

23. Schorske, interview with author.

24. Campbell, "History and Ethics."

25. Feldman, interview with author; Robert Tignor, telephone interview with author, January 1985.

26. Schorske, interview with author.

27. See for example Rick Bragg, "Fight Over Cuban Boy Leaves Scars in Miami," *New York Times,* June 30, 2000, A12.

6. Mike Davis and Power in Los Angeles

1. Portions of this chapter originally published as "L.A. Story: Backlash of the Boosters," *The Nation*, February 15, 1999, 19–21.

2. William Finnegan, "Earthquake Twister Inferno: The Sequel," review of *Ecology of Fear*, by Mike Davis, *New York Times Book Review*, August 23, 1998, 5; Eric Schine, "The Hellish Paradise That Is Los Angeles," review of *Ecology of Fear*, by Davis, *Business Week*, September 7, 1998, 16. See also John Leonard, "California Screaming," review of *Ecology of Fear*, by Davis, *The Nation*, October 5, 1998.

3. Nora Zamichow, "Apocalyptic Look at Los Angeles Sparks Literary Fistfight," *Los Angeles Times*, January 6, 1991, A1; Todd S. Purdum, "Best-Selling Author's Gloomy Future for Los Angeles Meets Resistance," *New York Times*, January 27, 1999, A10; "City of Frauds," *Economist*, December 12, 1998, 31, quoting Jill Stewart, "Peddling Fear," *New Times Los Angeles*, November 19–25, 1998.

4. D.J. Waldie, "Pornography of Despair," review of *Ecology of Fear*, by Davis, *Salon.com*, September 21, 1998; Greg Critser, "City of Self-Hate," *Salon.com*, December 15, 1998; Veronique de Turenne, "Is Mike Davis' Los Angeles All in his Head?" *Salon.com*, December 7, 1998; Stewart, "Peddling Fear"; Glenn Gaslin, "Fear This," *New Times Los Angeles*, December 3–9, 1998; Denise Hamilton, "The Gospel According to Mike," *New Times Los Angeles*, January 21–27, 1999, 10–19; Rick Barrs, "Ecology of Hype," *New Times Los Angeles*, January 21–27, 1999, 6; "Hit and Run CLVI," www.Suck.com/daily/1998/11/19, November 19, 1998; "Wall of Voodoo," www.Suck.com/daily/1998/12/14, December 14, 1998 (accessed May 11, 2004).

5. Mike Davis, *Ecology of Fear: Los Angeles and the Imagination of Disaster* (New York: Metropolitan Books, 1998), 9.

6. David Friedman, "The Ecology of Mike Davis," *Los Angeles Downtown News*, October 12, 1998; Mike Davis, interview with author, January 1999.

7. Brady Westwater, "Research Exposes . . . Mike Davis as Purposefully Misleading Liar," www.coagula.com/mike_davis.html (accessed March 17, 2004).

8. Purdum, "Gloomy Future."

9. Lewis MacAdams, "Jeremiah Among the Palms," *LA Weekly*, November 27–December 3, 1998, 25.

10. MacAdams, "Jeremiah Among the Palms," 25.

11. Sue Horton, telephone interview with author, January 1999; Mike Davis, interview with the author.

12. Sue Horton, interview with author.

13. Sue Horton, telephone interview with author.

14. De Turenne, "Is Mike Davis' Los Angeles All in his Head?"

15. Mike Davis, interview with author.

16. "Catellus Reports 82% Increase in Earnings Before Depreciation and Deferred Taxes per share in 1997 over 1996," *Business Wire,* January 29, 1998.

17. Purdum, "Gloomy Future."

18. Reason Foundation and Pepperdine: www.rppi.org/kotkin.html (accessed March 17, 2004).

19. Joel Kotkin, "The New Left Takes Over American Unions," *American Enterprise* 8:3 (May–June 1997), 58.

20. See Joel Kotkin and David Friedman, "California Porfolio: With a Friend like President Clinton, California Doesn't Need an Enemy," *Los Angeles Times,* June 27, 1993, M6; Joel Kotkin and David Friedman, "Put a Cork in It: As Wall Street Pats Itself on the Back, Trouble Lurks Behind the Boom," *Washington Post,* May 24, 1998, C01; Joel Kotkin and David Friedman, "Up? Down? Who Cares? The Dow Doesn't Mean Much," *Washington Post,* November 8, 1998, C01.

21. Purdum, "Gloomy Future."

22. Mike Davis, *City of Quartz: Excavating the Future in Los Angeles* (New York: Verso, 1990; New York: Vintage Books, 1992), 114. Citation is to the reprint edition.

23. See Thomas S. Hines, "Los Angeles and the Apocalyptic Tradition," review of *Ecology of Fear,* by Davis, *Los Angeles Times*, August 16, 1998, 3.

24. Zamichow, "Literary Fistfight," A1.

25. "City of Frauds," 31.

26. See Zamichow, "Literary Fistfight," A12.

27. "City of Frauds," 31; Friedman, "The Ecology of Mike Davis."

28. Mike Davis, interview with author. For figures on Los Angeles County population, state prisons, and welfare caseloads in Los Angeles County, see David Westphal, "Hispanic Residents on Move," *Modesto Bee,* September 4, 1998, A1; Dan Morain, "Davis Lowers Sights in His First Budget," *Los Angeles Times,* January 9, 1999, A1; Carla Rivera and Melissa Healy, "L.A. County Succeeding in Bid to Get Poor Off Aid," *Los Angeles Times,* August 20, 1998, A1.

29. Waldie, "Pornography of Despair."

30. Lisa Grant, telephone interview with author, January 1999.

31. Richard Walker, telephone interview with author, January 1999.

32. Kenneth Pomeranz quote at http://versobooks.com/books/cdef/d-titles/davis_
    m_late_victorian.shtml (accessed March 17, 2004). I'm on the history faculty
    at UC Irvine and joined the unanimous vote in favor of hiring Davis.

33. I'm indebted to Roy Rosenzweig for this insight.

34. Susan Salter Reynolds, "Mike Davis Makes a Mammoth Shift: The Iconoclas-
    tic Chronicler of Southern California Goes on an Arctic Adventure in His
    First Kids Book," *Los Angeles Times,* March 3, 2004, E1. That article, however,
    was full of errors. One faint shadow of the old *Los Angeles Times* appeared in a
    2004 story: media columnist Tim Rutten referred to Davis as "a gifted
    polemicist with a sometimes glancing appreciation of facts." Tim Rutten,
    "Regarding Media: Where Disaster Comes with the Geraniums," *Los Angeles
    Times,* October 29, 2003, E1.

7. The Denmark Vesey "Trial Record": A New Verdict

1. Edward A. Pearson, ed., *Designs against Charleston: The Trial Record of the Den-
   mark Vesey Slave Conspiracy of 1822* (Chapel Hill: University of North Carolina
   Press, 1999). Portions of this chapter originally published as "Denmark
   Vesey: A New Verdict," *The Nation,* March 1, 2002, 21–24.

2. Michael Johnson, "Denmark Vesey and His Co-Conspirators," *William and
   Mary Quarterly* 68:4 (October 2001), 915–71.

3. Edward A. Pearson, "Trials and Errors: Denmark Vesey and His Historians,"
   William and Mary Quarterly 69:1 (January 2002), 139.

4. Edward Pearson, e-mail to author, March 10, 2004.

5. Ira Berlin and Drew Gilpin Faust, quoted in the University of North Carolina
   Press catalogue for fall 1999 and on the press website. These quotes were removed after the book was withdrawn from publication.

6. Lorri Glover, review of *Designs against Charleston,* by Pearson, *Journal of American History* 88:2 (September 2001), 642–43.

7. Barbara L. Bellows, review of *Designs against Charleston,* by Pearson, *Journal of
   Southern History* 66:4 (Fall 2000), 862–63.

8. Randall M. Miller, review of *Designs against Charleston,* by Pearson, *North Carolina Historical Review* 76 (October 1999), 453.

9. Johnson, "Denmark Vesey," 925.

10. Ibid., 920–21.

11. Ibid., 921–33, 940n75.

12. Ibid., 933.

13. Ibid., 934.

14. Pearson, "Trials and Errors," 139.

15. Johnson, "Denmark Vesey," 956, quoting Lionel H. Kennedy and Thomas Parker, eds., *An Official Report of the Trials of Sundry Negroes, Charged with an Attempt to Raise an Insurrection in the State of South Carolina: Preceded by an Introduction and Narrative; and, in an Appendix, A Report of the Trials of Four White Persons on Indictments for Attempting to Excite the Slaves to Insurrection* (Charleston, 1822), 17.

16. Johnson, "Denmark Vesey," 933, 938, 956.

17. Ibid., 938, quoting Thomas Bennett, Jr., Message No. 2 to the Senate and House of Representatives of the State of South Carolina, November 28, 1822, Governor's Messages, 1328, General Assembly Papers, South Carolina Department of Archives and History.

18. Johnson, "Denmark Vesey," 936, quoting "Melancholy Effect of Popular Excitement," *Charleston Courier,* June 21, 1822.

19. Johnson, "Denmark Vesey," 936, quoting "Communication," *Charleston Courier,* June 29, 1822.

20. Johnson, "Denmark Vesey," 939.

21. Lou Morano, "The Slave Uprising That Wasn't," *United Press International,* November 7, 2001. Read online via Lexis-Nexis, March 2004.

22. William Johnson to Thomas Jefferson, August 11, 1823, in *South Carolina Historical and Genealogical Magazine* 1 (July 1900), 212, quoted in Robert L. Paquette, "Jacobins of the Low Country: The Vesey Plot on Trial," *William and Mary Quarterly* 59:1 (January 2002), 186.

23. Johnson, "Denmark Vesey," 971.

24. Douglas R. Egerton, "Forgetting Denmark Vesey; Or, Oliver Stone Meets Richard Wade," *William and Mary Quarterly* 59:1 (January 2002), 143–52; David Robertson, "Inconsistent Contextualism: The Hermeneutics of Michael Johnson," *William and Mary Quarterly* 59:1 (January 2002), 153–58; Edward Pearson, "Trials and Errors: Denmark Vesey and His Historians," *William and Mary Quarterly* 59:1 (January 2002), 137–42. For these historians' previous work on Vesey, see Douglas R. Egerton, *He Shall Go Out Free: The Lives of Denmark Vesey* (Madison, Wisconsin: Madison House, 1999); David Robertson, *Denmark Vesey* (New York: Alfred A. Knopf, 1999); Pearson, ed., *Designs against Charleston.* Pearson followed his apology with an argument that "even though my transcription of the trial document is inaccurate, the accompanying analysis . . . stands, I believe, as a sound piece of scholarship." Pearson, "Trials and

Errors," 139. Robert L. Paquette, "Jacobins of the Lowcountry: The Vesey Plot on Trial," *William and Mary Quarterly* 59:1 (January 2002), 185–92.

25. Winthrop Jordan, "The Charleston Hurricane of 1822; Or, the Law's Rampage," *William and Mary Quarterly* 59:1 (January 2002), 175, 178.

26. Philip D. Morgan, "Conspiracy Scares," *William and Mary Quarterly* 59:1 (January 2002), 160, 166.

27. Drew Gilpin Faust, telephone interview with author, February 2002.

28. James Sidbury, "Plausible Stories and Varnished Truths," *William and Mary Quarterly* 59:1 (January 2002), 179.

29. Peter Wood, telephone interview with author, February 2002.

30. Michael Johnson, telephone interview with author, February 2002.

31. Jason Hardin, "Experts on Vesey Still Agree to Disagree," *Charleston Post and Courier,* March 25, 2001, B1.

32. Jacqueline Jones, Peter H. Wood, Elaine Tyler May, Thomas Borstelmann, and Vicki L. Ruiz, *Created Equal: A Social and Political History of the United States* (New York: Longman, 2003), 379.

33. Dinitia Smith, "Challenging the History of a Slave Conspiracy," *New York Times,* February 23, 2002, B11. Also, I published an article about it: Jon Wiener, "Denmark Vesey: A New Verdict," *The Nation,* March 11, 2002, 21–24.

34. Joanne Meyerowitz, editor of the *JAH,* e-mail to author, June 27, 2003; "Historical Notes and Notions," *Journal of Southern History* 69:4 (November 2003), 1017; John Bowles, editor of the *JSH,* e-mail to author, June 27, 2003. The reviewer, Barbara Bellows, had not published any reconsideration in the *JSH* as of the February 2004 issue.

35. Edward Pearson, e-mail to author, March 10, 2004.

8. John Lott, Gun Rights, and Research Fraud

1. Bob von Sternberg, "Tough to Gauge: Concealed-Carry's Goal Is Less Crime, but There's No Consensus on Effect," *Minneapolis Star Tribune,* April 25, 2003, 1.

2. The report of 100,000 copies appears in Chris Mooney, "Double Barreled Double Standards," *Mother Jones,* September–October 2003, www.motherjones.com/news/feature/2003/10/we_590_01.html (accessed February 2, 2004). For a list of the states with "concealed carry" gun laws, see the website with the enthusiastic name "Packing.org": www.packing.org/state/report_basic.jsp?search=shall_issue (accessed March 17, 2004).

3. John R. Lott Jr., *More Guns, Less Crime* (Chicago: University of Chicago Press, 1998), 3.

4. Ibid.

5. John R. Lott Jr., "Childproof Gun Locks: Bound to Misfire," *Wall Street Journal,* July 16, 1997, A22; Lott, "Childproof Gun Locks: Bound to Misfire," *Chicago Tribune,* August 6, 1998; Lott, "Unraveling Some Brady Law Falsehoods," *Los Angeles Times,* July 2, 1997; Lott, "Packing Protection," Letters, *Chicago Sun-Times,* April 30, 1997, 52; Interview with Lott, *Dallas Morning News,* May 31, 1998; Lott, "Gun Regulations Can Cost Lives," Testimony before the House Judiciary Committee, May 27, 1999, www.house.gov/judiciary/lott.pdf (accessed March 17, 2004). See also "Statements by John R. Lott Jr. on Defensive Gun Brandishing," http://cgi.cse.unsw.edu.au/~lambert/cgi-bin/blog/guns/files/lottbrandish.html (accessed March 17, 2004).

6. Otis Dudley Duncan, "Gun Use Surveys: In Numbers We Trust?" *Criminologist* 25:1 (January/February 2000), 1–7, http://cgi.cse.unsw.edu.au/~lambert/cgi-bin/blog/guns/files/duncan1.html, cited by Lindgren, www.cse.unsw.edu.au/~lambert/guns/lindgren.html (both accessed March 26, 2004).

7. John R. Lott Jr., *More Guns, Less Crime,* 2nd ed. (Chicago: University of Chicago Press, 2000), 3.

8. Tim Lambert: http://cgi.cse.unsw.edu.au/~lambert/cgi-bin/blog/ (accessed March 17, 2004).

9. Lindgren, "Comments on Questions About John R. Lott's Claims Regarding a 1997 Survey," http://.cse.unsw.edu.au/~lambert/guns/lindgren.html (accessed March 17, 2004).

10. Ibid.

11. Ibid.

12. Timothy Noah, "The Bellesiles of the Right? Another Firearms Scholar Whose Dog Ate His Data," *Slate.com,* February 3, 2003, http://slate.msn.com/id/2078084/ (accessed March 20, 2004).

13. That was what Tim Lambert suggested: Lambert, "Cramer's Defense of Lott," October 24, 2003, at Lambert's blog: http://cgi.cse.unsw.edu.au/~lambert/cgi-bin/blog/2003/10 (accessed March 27, 2004).

14. Richard Morin, "Scholar Invents Fan to Answer His Critics," *Washington Post,* February 1, 2003, C1.

15. Mark Stamaty, "BOOX: Pity the Poor Gun," *New York Times Book Review,* March 2, 2003, 31. The image can be found at www.nytimes.com/

imagepages/2003/03/02/books/20030302stamaty.html (accessed February 3, 2004).

16. David Glenn, "Scholar's Most Vigorous Defender Turns Out to be Himself, Psuedonymously," *Chronicle of Higher Education,* February 14, 2003, 18; Noah, "The Bellesiles of the Right?"; Ron Grossman, "Another Misfire in the Academic Shootout on Guns," *Chicago Tribune,* February 14, 2003, C1; Mooney, "Double Barreled Double Standards."

17. Lott, letter to the editor, *Washington Post,* March 22, 2003, A15. Lott was repying to a brief item that contained one sentence reporting that he denied "faking evidence": Claudia Deane and Richard Morin, "A Fabricated Fan and Many Doubts," *Washington Post,* February 11, 2003, A19.

18. The statement was made by David Mustard to Lindgren, reported at www.cse.unsw.edu.au/~lambert/guns/lindgren.html (accessed January 31, 2004).

19. www.johnlott.org, see "General Discussion of the 1997 and 2002 Surveys," notes 14 and 15.

20. Lott, untitled statement, www.johnlott.org/files/GenDisc97_02surveys.html (accessed January 29, 2004).

21. David Hemenway, review of *The Bias Against Guns: Why Almost Everything You've Heard About Gun Control Is Wrong,* by John Lott Jr., at Harvard School of Public Health website, www.hsph.harvard.edu/faculty/ Hemenway/book.html (accessed February 2, 2004).

22. John R. Lott Jr. and David B Mustard, "Crime, Deterrence, and Right-to-Carry Concealed Handguns," *Journal of Legal Studies* 26 (1997), 65.

23. The evidence, originally critiqued in Dan Black and Daniel Nagin, "Do Right-to-Carry Laws Deter Violent Crime?" *Journal of Legal Studies* 27:1 (1998), 209–19, is summarized in Mooney, "Double Barreled Double Standards."

24. Ian Ayres and John J. Donohue III, "Shooting Down the 'More Guns, Less Crime' Hypothesis," *Stanford Law Review* 55:4 (April 2003), 1371–98. See also John J. Donohue III, "The Impact of Concealed Carry Laws," in Jens Ludwig and Philip J. Cook, eds., *Evaluating Gun Policy: Effects on Crime and Violence* (Washington: Brookings Institution, 2003), www.brookings.edu/dybdocroot/ press/books/chapter_1/evaluatinggunpolicy.pdf (accessed February 3, 2004). Lott of course defended his work with a variety of complicated but unsuccessful arguments, which are reviewed in Mooney, "Double Barreled Double Standards."

25. See Jon Wiener, "Dollars for Neocon Scholars: The Olin Money Tree," *The Nation,* January 1, 1990, 12–14.

26. For Lott's webpage at the American Enterprise Institute, see www.aei.org/scholars/scholarID.38/scholar.asp (accessed February 3, 2004).

27. Nexis search conducted January 27, 2004.

28. The same problem is evident in the work of James Lindgren, the Northwestern law professor who worked on both the Bellesiles and the Lott cases. The differences in his efforts in the two cases are striking. He published 122 pages on the Bellesiles case in two journal articles with a total of 436 footnotes. He gave more than a dozen public lectures on the Bellesiles case at universities and law schools including Yale, Columbia, Chicago, Berkeley, William and Mary, and Penn. He contacted reviewers of the Bellesiles book and repeatedly urged them to publish reconsiderations. (See chapter 4)

    He didn't do any of this with his work documenting Lott's deception. It was not published anywhere, and it's not even posted on his website—where his Bellesiles materials are still proudly reproduced. Indeed the only place readers can find Lindgren's work on the Lott case is the website of Tim Lambert at the University of New South Wales. There Lindgren can be found stating "I have no research interests in this subfield and no ideas for further efforts to get to the bottom of this inquiry. . . . This project detracts from my other scholarly efforts"—and declaring he was not going to do any more on it. Compare www.law.nwu.edu/faculty/fulltime/Lindgren/Lindgren.html with www.cse.unsw.edu.au/~lambert/guns/lindgren.html (both accessed January 31, 2004), and see Lindgren, "Personal Note, January 17, 2003," www.cse.unsw.edu.au/~lambert/guns/lindgren.html (accessed January 31, 2004).

29. Clayton Cramer, who devoted immense energies to attacking Bellesiles, defends Lott: "*Mother Jones* on the Lott Controversy," undated, at Cramer's blog, http://claytoncramer.com/weblog/2003_10_12_archive.html#106605679596614813 (accessed March 27, 2004). For a critique see Lambert, "Cramer's Defense of Lott." See also Noah, "The Bellesiles of the Right?"

30. For some recent examples of Lott's continuing work, see his characteristic piece "Baghdad's Murder Rate Irresponsibly Distorted," *Investor's Business Daily,* December 12, 2003, A14; also "The Spin on Gun Control," *Washington Times,* November 14, 2003, A23; and the most surprising venue, "Many Experts Agree: Concealed Guns Cut Crime," *Madison Capital Times,* September 8, 2003, 9A.

9. The "Porn Professor": Dino Cinel, Sexual Abuse, and the Catholic Church

1. Portions of this chapter originally published as "Sex, Lies and Tenure: The Porn Prof on Trial," *The Nation,* November 8, 1993, 524–28.
2. Robert V. Wolf, "Professor Teaches the History He Has Lived," *Staten Island Advance,* February 25, 1991, B1; "CSI Welcomes Distinguished Professor," *Staten Island Advance,* April 8, 1991, A6. Cinel's qualifications seemed impressive: his book, *From Italy to San Francisco* (Stanford University Press, 1982) won the Merle Curti Award in Social History for 1984, and he gave the opening address at the 1989 American Italian Historical Association conference in San Francisco for an exhibit titled "Shattering the Stereotype." The book was later shown to be based on fraudulent research: Sebastian Fichera, "The Disturbing Case of Dino Cinel," *History News Network,* April 28, 2003, http://hnn.us/articles/1420.html (accessed March 13, 2004).
3. Brian Larkin, "CSI Prof Admits Sex Scandals," *Staten Island Advance,* May 16, 1991, A1.
4. Ibid.; Steve Cannizaro, "Cinel's Lawsuit Updated," *New Orleans Times-Picayune,* April 15, 1992, B4.
5. Brian Larkin, "CUNY Acting on Sex Prof," *Staten Island Advance,* January 14, 1992, A1.
6. Brian Larkin, "Judge Cans CSI Prof's Porn Charges," *Staten Island Advance,* January 11, 1992, A1.
7. Brian Larkin, "CSI Prof Admits Sex Scandal," *Staten Island Advance,* May 16, 1991, A1; the "spectre of McCarthyism" was argued by CUNY history professor Sandi Cooper, interview with author, October 1993.
8. Nick Russo, telephone interview with author, October 1993.
9. "General University Policy Regarding Academic Appointees: Faculty Conduct and Administration of Discipline, Including the Faculty Code of Conduct," *University of California Academic Personnel Manual* (rev. September 1, 1988), 12.
10. Leslie Bennetts, "Unholy Alliances," *Vanity Fair,* December 1991, 224; Jason Berry, *Lead Us Not into Temptation: Catholic Priests and the Sexual Abuse of Children* (New York: Doubleday, 1992), 296–97.
11. Berry, *Lead Us Not into Temptation,* 294.
12. Ray Bigelow, telephone interview with author, October 1993; Richard Angelico, telephone interview with author, October 1993.
13. Ernst Benjamin, telephone interview with author, October 1993.
14. Richard Gid Powers, telephone interview with author, October 1993.

15. Steve Cannizaro, "Ex-priest Sues District Attorney," *New Orleans Times-Picayune,* February 28, 1992, B8; see also Berry, *Lead Us Not into Temptation,* 297.

16. Bennetts, "Unholy Alliances," 228, 274.

17. Ibid. 274.

18. August 9, 1990, deposition of Dino Cinel at 106:7–9, taken in *Fontaine v. Roman Catholic Church of the Archdiocese of New Orleans,* No. 89-25790 (La. Civ. Dist. Ct.); Russo, telephone interview with author.

19. David Nasaw, telephone interview with author, September 2003. Nasaw was search committee chair.

20. Matt Finkin, telephone interview with author, October 1993.

21. Nasaw, interview with author.

22. Deposition of Dino Cinel at 98:7–25; 99:1–10.

23. Brian Larkin, "CSI Prof Admits Sex Scandals."

24. Bennetts, "Unholy Alliances," 270.

25. Ibid. 228.

26. Irwin Polishook, telephone interview with author, October 1993.

27. Berry, interview with author. See also Berry, *Lead Us Not into Temptation,* 291–98; Thomas M. Disch, "The Sins of the Fathers," review of *Lead Us Not into Temptation,* by Berry, *The Nation,* November 2, 1992, 514–16.

28. Gary Raymond, telephone interview with author, October 1993.

29. Sandi Cooper, telephone interview with author, October 1993.

30. Brian Larkin, "CSI Acting to Oust Porn Prof," *Staten Island Advance,* July 15, 1991, A1; Brian Larkin, "CUNY Press Job for Sex Prof," *Staten Island Advance,* September 7, 1991, A1.

31. Ron Grossman, "Academic Exile: N.Y. Professor's Past Comes Back with a Vengeance," *Chicago Tribune,* December 22, 1993, Tempo section, 1.

32. James Varney, "Jury Set for Trial Of Ex-Priest," *New Orleans Times-Picayune,* August 22, 1995, A1. Later that year, in Cinel's New Orleans trial for possession of child pornography, a jury found him not guilty after he testified that he had been molested as a child by a priest. Calvin Baker, "Ex-Priest Innocent on Porn Charges," *New Orleans Times-Picayune,* August 25, 1995, A1. A month after that, the *Times-Picayune* revealed that the judge, the jury foreman, and Cinel's attorney were all members of Cinel's former parish church and "knew each other well." The jury foreman had also been defended by Cinel's attorney when he was charged in a "scam . . . to con money from homosexuals." James Varney, "Cinel Trial Judge, Juror, Lawyer Linked," *New Orleans Times-Picayune,* September 15, 1995, A1; James Gill, "The Cinel Saga," *New Orleans*

Times-Picayune, September 17, 1995, B7. The civil suits were settled by the Church for an undisclosed amount without coming to trial. Bill Voelker, "N.O. Archdiocese Settles Nude-Photo Suit," *New Orleans Times-Picayune,* February 15, 1995, B3.

33. Nasaw, interview with author.

34. Sebastian Fichera, "The Disturbing Case of Dino Cinel," *History News Network,* April 28, 2003, http://hnn.us/articles/1420.html (accessed March 26, 2004).

35. "CUNY Settles Suit by Italian Institute," *New York Times,* January 9, 1994, 1, 22.

10. Lying to Students About Vietnam: The Mythic Past of Joseph Ellis

1. Walter V. Robinson, "Professor's Past In Doubt," *Boston Globe,* June 18, 2001, A1.

2. Ibid.

3. Ibid.

4. Ibid.

5. Ibid.

6. Ibid.

7. Ibid.

8. Ibid.

9. Ibid.

10. Ibid.

11. "Notebook," *New Republic,* July 2, 2001, 8.

12. "The Lying Historian" (editorial), *New York Post,* June 23, 2001, 14.

13. Garrow himself would be disciplined by Emory in 2003, for assaulting a staff member. See chapter 1, 26–28.

14. David J. Garrow, "Ellis Broke Golden Rule at Teaching," *Boston Globe,* June 20, 2001, A13.

15. Garrow quoted in Josh Tyrangiel, "A History of His Own Making," *Time,* July 2, 2001, 52; Lynn Smith and Tim Rutten, "For Historian's Students, a Hard Lesson on Lying," *Los Angeles Times,* June 22, 2001, A1; Sheryl McCarthy, "Professor Who Lied Is Too Brilliant to Sacrifice," *New York Newsday,* June 25, 2001, A22; "What Was He Thinking?" (editorial), *Chicago Tribune,* June 28, 2001, 28.

16. Pamela Ferdinand, "A Historian's Embellished Life; Joseph Ellis Took Metic-

ulous Care with Facts–Except His Own Story," *Washington Post,* June 23, 2001, C1.

17. Green quoted in Smith and Rutten, "A Hard Lesson on Lying."

18. Jack Beatty, "Politics and Prose," *Atlantic Unbound,* July 6, 2001, www. theatlantic.com/unbound/polipro/pp2001-07-05.htm (accessed March 17, 2004).

19. Ibid.

20. Ibid.

21. Ibid.

22. Geneva Overholser, "Media Got Condit, Ellis Right," *Seattle Post-Intelligencer,* July 13, 2001, B7.

23. David Abel, "College Suspends History Professor; Ellis's Lying Brought 'Hurt,' President Says," *Boston Globe,* August 18, 2001, A1.

24. Ibid.

25. Ibid. The three were William T. Whitely, a business professor at the University of Oklahoma, who resigned after admitting that "he had lied on his resume and to students in his classes about having been a Navy SEAL"; Larry E. Cable, a tenured professor of history at the University of North Carolina, Wilmington, who "resigned shortly after a local newspaper found that he had fabricated his Vietnam record"; and Joachim Maitre, dean of the Boston University School of Communications, who "resigned not long after the *Globe* reported that he had used as part of his commencement speech portions of a previously published article by film critic Michael Medved."

26. "Prof. Ellis' Punishment" (editorial), *Hartford Courant,* September 10, 2001, A10.

27. Joseph J. Ellis, "The Big Man: History vs. Alexander Hamilton," *New Yorker,* October 29, 2001, 76.

28. Judith Shulevitz, "The Wound and the Historian," *New York Times Book Review,* July 15, 2001, 31.

29. Ibid. For a similar view, see Joyce Lee Malcolm, "Disarming History," *Reason,* March 2003, 25. Malcolm teaches history at Bentley College and is a gun historian and critic of Bellesiles.

30. "The Lies of Joseph Ellis" (editorial), *New York Times,* August 21, 2001, A16.

31. Joseph J. Ellis, "Exploring the Morning of a Long Day's Journey," review of *O'Neill,* by Arthur Gelb and Barbara Gelb, *New York Times,* May 19, 2000, 45; Joseph J. Ellis, "Clash of the Titans," review of *What Kind of Nation,* by James F. Simon, *New York Times Book Review,* March 10, 2002, 10. The *Times Book Re-*

view continued to feature him the next year, with the shortened ID: Joseph J. Ellis, "The Many-Minded Man," review of *Benjamin Franklin: An American Life,* by Walter Isaacson, *New York Times Book Review,* July 6, 2003, 11.

11. The Plagiarists: Doris Kearns Goodwin and Stephen Ambrose

1. Thomas C. Palmer Jr., "Goodwin Discloses Settlement Over Credits," *Boston Globe,* January 22, 2002, A1. See also David D. Kirkpatrick, "Historian Says Publisher Quickly Settled Copying Dispute," *New York Times,* January 23, 2002, A10.

2. Lynne McTaggart, "Fame Can't Excuse a Plagiarist," *New York Times,* March 16, 2002, A15; Timothy Noah, "Goodwin's Tribe: A Harvard Law Professor Chides the *Crimson* for Criticizing a Plagiarist," *Slate.com,* March 18, 2002, http://slate.msn.com/?id=2063299 (accessed March 19, 2004).

3. Bo Crader, "Lynne McTaggart on Doris Kearns Goodwin," *Daily Standard,* January 23, 2002, www.theweekly-standard.com/Content/Public/Articles/000/000/000/817/duk.asp (accessed March 19, 2004). See also "Purloined Letters," *USA Today,* February 27, 2002, www.usatoday.com/news/opinion/2002/02/27/edtwof2.htm (accessed March 19, 2004).

4. Palmer, "Goodwin Discloses Settlement"; Crader, "McTaggart on Goodwin."

5. Doris Kearns Goodwin, "How I Caused That Story," *Time,* February 4, 2002, 69, www.time.com/time/nation/article/0,8599,197614,00.html (accessed March 19, 2004).

6. Arthur Schlesinger Jr. et al., letter to the editor, *New York Times,* October 25, 2003; additional signers listed at *History News Network,* http://hnn.us/articles/1195.html#doris10-27-03 (accessed March 10, 2003).

7. David D. Kirkpatrick, "Historian's Fight for Her Reputation May Be Damaging It," *New York Times,* March 31, 2002, A18.

8. See for example *Hardball,* February 16, 2004, MSNBC transcript on Lexis-Nexis; *The News on CNBC,* January 20, 2004, CNBC transcript on Lexis-Nexis and *Meet the Press,* February 29, 2004, NBC News transcript on Lexis-Nexis (all accessed March 19, 2004).

9. Thomas Bartlett, "Naval Academy Demotes Professor Accused of Plagiarism in a Book on the A-bomb," *Chronicle of Higher Education,* November 7, 2003, 12; Maurice Isserman, "Plagiarism: A Lie of the Mind," *Chronicle of Higher Education,* May 2, 2003, 12; Sharon Walsh, "SUNY-Albany Classicist Loses

Chairmanship After Being Accused of Plagiarism," *Chronicle of Higher Education,* March 8, 2002, 12.

10. For a good report on Ambrose, see Coleman Warner, "Under Fire," *New Orleans Times-Picayune,* March 31, 2002, www.nola.com/news/t-p/frontpage/index.ssf?/newsstory/ambrose31(2).html (accessed March 18, 2004).

11. Matthew Rose, "History Inc. As a Professor's Books become Bestsellers, a Big Business is Born," *Wall Street Journal,* August 20, 2001.

12. Ibid. For the tour ad, see http://hnn.us/articles/504.html#latest (accessed March 18, 2004).

13. Fred Barnes, "Now, Stephen Ambrose," *Weekly Standard,* January 9, 2002, http://historynewsnetwork.org/articles/article.html?id=499 (accessed March 17, 2004).

14. David D. Kirkpatrick, "Author Admits He Lifted Lines From '95 Book," *New York Times,* January 6, 2002, A22; Fred Barnes, "Ambrose Apologizes," *Weekly Standard,* January 7, 2002, www.weeklystandard.com/Content/Public/Articles/000/000/000/752brzuv.asp (accessed March 18, 2004).

15. Mark Lewis, "Did Ambrose Write Wild Blue, or Just Edit It?" *Forbes.com,* February 27, 2002, www.forbes.com/2002/02/27/0227ambrose.html (accessed March 20, 2004).

16. George McGovern, letter to the editor, *New York Times,* January 28, 2002, A14. McGovern's letter appeared before *Forbes.com* presented evidence that Ambrose had plagiarized from McGovern's memoir.

17. Richard Jensen, "The Plagiarism Problem," *OAH Newsletter,* August 2002, www.oah.org/pubs/nl/2002aug/jensen.html, cited in Michael Grossberg, "Plagiarism and Professional Ethics—A Journal Editor's View," *Journal of American History* 90:4 (March 2004), www.historycooperative.org/journals/jah/90.4/grossberg.html (both accessed March 9, 2004).

18. The whole story is summed up at http://hnn.us/articles/504.html#latest (accessed March 17, 2004).

19. "Newsmakers: Ambrose Writing Last War Book," *Houston Chronicle,* February 24, 2002, A2.

20. Megan Stack, "For Historian Ambrose, It's Time for a 'Love Song,'" *Los Angeles Times,* May 11, 2002, A1.

21. Richard Pearson, "Stephen Ambrose Dies; Popular U.S. Historian," *Washington Post,* October 14, 2002, B7, www.washingtonpost.com/ac2/wp-dyn?pagename=article&node=&contentId=A21907-2002Oct13&notFound=true (accessed March 17, 2004).

22. Richard Goldstein, "Stephen Ambrose, Historian Who Fueled New Interest in World War II, Dies at 66," *New York Times,* October 14, 2002, B7.

23. "Statement on Plagiarism," *Perspectives: Newsmagazine of the American Historical Association,* March 2002, www.theaha.org/perspectives/issues/2002/0203/0203aha4.cfm (accessed March 18, 2004).

24. Barbara D. Metcalf, "Lessons from the Professional Division: Complaints Concerning Plagiarism," *Perspectives: Newsmagazine of the American Historical Association,* September 2001, www.theaha.org/perspectives/issues/2001/0111/0111pro1.cfm (accessed March 18, 2004).

25. Ron Robin, *Scandals and Scoundrels,* 11; Lears quoted in Jay Tolson, "Whose Own Words?" *U.S. News and World Report,* January 21, 2002, 52, www.usnews.com/usnews/issue/archive/020121/20020121020041_brief.php (accessed March 18, 2004).

26. Robin, *Scandals and Scoundrels,* 23–24.

27. Nicholas Confessore, "Selling Private Ryan; Stephen Ambrose, Tom Brokaw, Steven Spielberg, and the Abuse of Nostalgia," *American Prospect,* September 24, 2001, 21, www.prospect.org/print/V12/17/confessore-n.html (accessed March 18, 2004).

28. Benjamin Schwarz, "The Real War: Stephen Ambrose's GIs Are Plaster Saints Engaged in a Sanctified Crusade," *Atlantic* 287, June 2001, 100–103, www.theatlantic.com/issues/2001/06/noteworthy.htm (accessed March 18, 2004).

29. Robin, *Scandals and Scoundrels,* 11.

30. The Sokolow story is the subject of chapter 4, "Quiet Goes the Don," in Thomas Mallon, *Stolen Words* (New York: Penguin Books, 1991), 144–93; "sloppy notetaking" appears on 169.

31. Ibid.

32. Ibid., 176–77.

33. Ibid. 179.

34. Sokolow's letter appeared in the *American Historical Review* 90 (February 1985), 274; see Mallon, *Stolen Words,* 185–86.

35. Quoted in Mallon, *Stolen Words,* 183–84.

36. Quoted in Ibid., 185.

37. "Statement on Plagiarism," *Perspectives: Newsmagazine of the American Historical Association,* October 1986, 7.

38. Stephen Nissenbaum, "The Plagiarists in Academe Must Face Formal Sanctions," *Chronicle of Higher Education,* March 28, 1990, A48.

39. Thomas Mallon went on to publish several critically acclaimed novels, including *Bandbox* (2004), *Henry and Clara* (1994), and *Dewey Defeats Truman* (1997). He is a frequent contributor to the *Atlantic Monthly,* the *New Yorker,* and other magazines.

Conclusion

1. Thomas Bartlett, "Historical Assocation Will No Longer Investigate Allegations of Wrongdoing," *Chronicle of Higher Education,* May 23, 2003, 12.
2. "Statement on Standards of Professional Conduct," www.historians.org/pubs/ Free/ProfessionalStandards.htm (accessed March 30, 2004).
3. William J. Cronon, "A Watershed for the Professional Division," *Perspectives: Newsmagazine of the American Historical Association* 41:6 (September 2003), 16–18, www.theaha.org/perspectives/issues/2003/0309/0309aha1.cfm (accessed March 18, 2004).
4. Bartlett, "Historical Assocation Will No Longer Investigate."
5. Those who criticized the decision included Carla Rahn Phillips, a professor at the University of Minnesota, Twin Cities, who had preceded Cronon as head of the Professional Division, from 1996 to 1999. "I happen to believe that plagiarism is one of the worst violations of professional standards, certainly in the history profession, and I would be loath to see a time when individuals have no recourse against this," she told the *Chronicle.* Quoted in Ibid.
6. "Book Reviewing in the *AHR,*" www.historycooperative.org/ahr/guidebkrv. html (accessed March 17, 2004). See also Grossberg, "Plagiarism."
7. Grossberg, "Plagiarism"; Richard Posner, "On Plagiarism: In the Wake of Recent Scandals Some Distinctions Are in Order," *Atlantic Online,* April 2002, www.theatlantic.com/issues/2002/04/posner.htm (accessed March 9, 2004), quoted in Grossberg, "Plagiarism."
8. Grossberg, "Plagiarism."
9. Elliot J. Gorn, "The Historians' Dilemma," *Journal of American History* 90:4 (March 2004), 1327.
10. David Callahan, *The Cheating Culture: Why More Americans Are Doing Wrong to Get Ahead* (New York: Harcourt, 2004), 21, 23.
11. Gorn, "Historians' Dilemma," 1328.
12. Stone, interview with author.

13. For example, Richard Wightman Fox writes, "I doubt there is any more intellectual fraud among historians today than there was in the past." Fox, "A Heartbreaking Problem of Staggering Proportions," *Journal of American History* 90:4 (March 2004), 1341.

14. Robin, *Scandals and Scoundrels,* 10.

15. Ibid., 9.

16. This statement is based on a search of the Lexis-Nexis news database, which includes the *Chronicle of Higher Education.* Of course the *History News Network* website contains many vitriolic comments about Bellesiles, but the overwhelming majority of these were not posted by faculty members at colleges or universities, but rather by gun rights activists, some of whom work as independent scholars, like Clayton Cramer.

17. David J. Garrow, "Ellis Broke Golden Rule of Teaching," *Boston Globe,* June 20, 2001, A13. Garrow on Bellesiles quoted in Jen Sansbury, "Emory Professor's Book 'Biased,' Peers Say," *Atlanta Journal-Constitution*, February 10, 2002, 1C.

Update

1. U.S. Senate Governmental Affairs Committee, Hearing, July 22, 2004, transcript at www.lexis.com; Bruce Craig, "Special Report—The Confirmation Hearing of Allen Weinstein," *NCH Washington Update* 10, no. 32 (July 23, 2004), www2.h-net.msu.edu/~nch (accessed August 7, 2004); see also George Lardner Jr., "Archivist's Resignation Questioned; Democrats Seek Reason for His Being Pushed Out," *Washington Post*, July 26, 2004, A17.

Index